LOTUS
The Legend

LOTUS
The Legend

David Hodges

Page 1: The Lotus badge, first seen on a car in 1951, incorporates the founder's initials, Anthony Colin Bruce Chapman. Page 2: Elise is a sports car, thoroughly modern in concept yet recalling the marque's early cars. Page 3: Esprit V8, the long-awaited V8-powered Lotus that appeared in 1996. Page 5: The Eleven set new sports-racing car standards in the 1950s.

This is a Parragon Book

© Parragon 1997
Reprinted in 1998

Parragon Publishing
13 Whiteladies Road
Clifton
Bristol BS8 1P8

Designed, produced and packaged by
Touchstone
Old Chapel Studio, Plain Road, Marden,
Tonbridge, Kent TN12 9LS, United Kingdom

Edited by Philip de Ste. Croix

ISBN 0-75252-074-1

Printed in Italy

About this book

The theme of this book is Lotus road cars, but necessarily with more than a nod towards the racing cars that have been so important in the marque's history. A final chapter recalls four great Lotus Grand Prix cars.

Photographic credits:

All photographs by **Neill Bruce Motoring Photolibrary**, with the exception of the following: *(Abbreviations: r = right, l = left, t = top, b = below)*

Mrs Hazel Chapman: 6(*r*).

The Lotus Group Archive & The Peter Roberts Collection with Neill Bruce: 9(*b*), 12(*b*), 14(*t*), 15, 40, 43(*b*), 45(*b*), 46-47, 49, 50-51, 52, 56(*t*), 57, 59(*r*), 62-63, 66, 67(*t*), 68(*r*), 69, 71, 75(*b*), 77.

David Hodges Collection: 6(*l*), 7(*t*), 7(*b*), 8(*l*), 8(*r*), 12(*t*), 13, 14(*b*), 35(*b*), 37(*b*), 48, 56(*b*), 59(*l*), 76, 78, 79.

The GP library: 29.

Mick Walsh, Classic & Sportscar Magazine: 10-11, 41.

Andrew Morland: 23.

Figures and data in this book are quoted in metric measurements first, with the Imperial equivalents noted in brackets.

Neill Bruce and the publishers would like to thank all the owners who have made their cars available for photography, especially the following:

Brooks Auctioneers: Mark VI, first Elan and racing Eleven (green).

Graham Nearn and the Caterham Collection: Sevens series 1, 2 and 3.

Nigel Dawes: Team and road Elites and gullwing Eleven.

The Earl of March for the wonderful Goodwood Festival of Speed.

Special thanks to all the staff in the Lotus Press Office, and especially Jim Corbett, who spent two days with Neill on the Esprit V8 and Elise photography.

Contents

Introduction

FOR MANY years the story of Lotus centred on Colin Chapman, and it still reflects that outstanding man in many ways. His first Lotus was an Austin Seven 'special' and through the next thirty years he built up a complex modern company, and one of the most famous of all Grand Prix teams. His personal abilities were prodigious. He had a rare ability to grasp the essence of a problem, to master principles or details; he was imaginative and almost invariably his cars were innovative; he was able to communicate thoughts to his highly-talented designers, researchers, engineers and mechanics, and motivate them.

Above: Colin Chapman favoured check shirts in the 1950s.

Yet he could obstinately follow a false trail, and distractions, for example into power boat manufacture in the early 1970s or microlight aircraft projects a decade on, when Lotus affairs demanded his full attention – he was chief executive of a car company, and for years he was manager of a Grand Prix team, and was the inspiration and design trouble-shooter for both.

Colin Chapman often faced enormous commercial problems, and his business philosophies might have been rated sharp, his practices sometimes verging on questionable, but his marque survived hard times. It also survived his early death, after a heart attack in December 1982, and the mystique of Lotus is still strong . . .

Eventful Half Century

In the years immediately after the Second World War, two students at University College, London, bought and sold small cars as a sideline. Chapman's partner in this wheeler-dealer business 'retired' in 1947, and late that year the market collapsed under him. Eventually, he reduced his stock to an unsaleable 1930 Austin Seven, which he started to rebuild before deciding to make a trials car out of it. This was to be completed in a garage belonging to the father of his girlfriend Hazel Williams, whom he was to marry in 1954. He chose to call this car 'Lotus Mk I' – the reason was never explained, save that he did not want it known as another Austin Special.

National Service in the RAF meant that Lotus Mk II took shape slowly through 1949; he competed with it at Silverstone in June 1950, and that gave him a new passion.

Right: Chapman in a Lotus Mk II in 1949, with Hazel Williams as his passenger. Below: Racing a Mk VI in 1953.

Lotus entered a new phase with the III. This also started life as a one-off special (for 750 Formula racing), but a replica was built, then the IIIB for 1100cc racing. It was the first car to carry the badge that was to become famous, incorporating an ACBC monogram (Anthony Colin Bruce Chapman).

Another III was built, then another trials car. The car operation now carried on in the old stables behind his father's pub in North London was still a second occupation for Chapman – he did not leave British Aluminium until 1954 and for a while had two full-time professional jobs – so his partner

Left: Landmark design – the backbone chassis of the first Elan, forked at the front to embrace the engine, and at the rear to the Chapman strut suspension mountings.

Above: Lotus' first purpose-built factory, at Cheshunt, with a quintet of Lotus-Cortinas showing the company's growing stature. The building was already crowded.

Michael Allen was Lotus' first full-time worker. On the first day of 1952 Lotus Engineering was formed, and that year Chapman designed the Mk 6. In 1953 it was 'in production', so it is the first Lotus profiled in this book.

That year Mike Costin joined, on a part-time basis until 1955. He was to become technical director before he left in 1962, some time after he had formed Cosworth Engineering with another talented and highly practical designer who also spent time with Lotus, Keith Duckworth.

Lotus Cars Limited came into being in 1955.

The demand for its aerodynamic sports-racers and kits for the chunky Seven meant that the stables became very congested, and Lotus moved to a purpose-built factory at Cheshunt in 1959; it was to be the base through a period of commercial and racing success, but Lotus soon started to outgrow it. For a new site, Chapman looked for a disused military airfield – apart from land for buildings, this could provide facilities for his own aviation and a test track. He settled on the 22.5 hectare (55 acre) one-time USAF base at Hethel near Norwich, and Lotus completed another move late in 1966.

Above: In the early 1960s Les Leston raced an Elite registered DAD 10 with great success on British circuits, often in competition with Graham Warner in an Elite registered LOV 1. Leston's car had aerodynamic improvements devised for Le Mans around the nose, as seen on this car at Goodwood in 1993. Left: Chapman with the first Seven in 1957.

Mk III was significant in the Lotus story, despite lingering Austin 7 origins, for Michael and Nigel Allen built duplicates, while Chapman turned to Mk IV and Mk VI. This car is the IIIB, built for a customer, with cleaner bodywork. The cockpit (far left) was typically spartan, while the cleverly-modified Ford engine was squeezed in (left). The Lotus badge appeared for the first time on the III (below). The rear three-quarters view (right) shows odd bulges. The driver with the IIIB in full flight some 45 years after it was built is Mick Walsh of Classic and Sports Car.

Meanwhile, as Cheshunt opened, Lotus Components Limited had been formed, to look after customer racing cars and the Seven. It was to last until 1972, for its final two years as Lotus Racing, and run from 1969 by the energetic Mike Warner. He was soon disenchanted. The Seven did not fit into Chapman's scheme to move Lotus up-market, and there was little or no profit in building racing cars for sale, so both were abandoned.

More positively, Tony Rudd joined from BRM in 1969, and was soon to become Technical Director and be responsible for real progress on the production car side.

Lotus was floated as a public company, and that proved to be a mixed blessing. For all his business activities, Chapman was not a natural tycoon, and in the 1970s he was to spend more time away from Hethel, at nearby Ketteringham Hall, where his design department, research and development unit, and Team Lotus, were based.

In the mid-1970s sales were poor, and while Chapman was to become preoccupied with Team Lotus for a while, he looked to design and engineering consultancy to provide compensating income for Lotus Cars, as he would again in the early 1980s (Lotus Engineering and Technology was

Opposite top: The crowded Elan 'production lines' at Cheshunt. Lotus had moved to this purpose-built factory in 1959. Opposite below: An 'active suspension' Esprit cornering hard, but showing negligible roll.

COLLABORATION

Since it moved to its purpose-built Hethel plant, and probably while it was still at Cheshunt, Lotus has never built enough cars to support a realistic new-model programme. So, rather than attempt to grow out of being a modest manufacturer, it has worked with and for majors, adapted some others' products, and has been owned by one of the largest automobile companies and more recently by one of the smallest. The formation of the Lotus Engineering and Technology unit as such was announced late in 1980, and Lotus Engineering has been more important to the Group than Lotus Cars products for two decades . . .

● The Twin Cam engine based on a Ford block was built for 11 years from 1962.

● The Ford Lotus-Cortina saloon was built by Lotus, 1962-66 (see page 36); it was followed by the Cortina II Lotus (1967-70), where the association was nominal.

● The LV engine using a Vauxhall block, intended for racing in LV220 2-litre form, appeared in 1968; the 1971 Lotus 907 intended for road car use derived from it.

● The De Lorean DMC-2 design and development agreement was signed in 1978, and cars showed the benefits of Lotus chassis and suspension input when they appeared in 1981. But John Z De Lorean's project foundered a year later, in scandalous financial circumstances which touched some Lotus executives.

● Chrysler (UK) contracted Lotus to contribute to the development of the Talbot Sunbeam Lotus from 1978; this car was powered by a Lotus 2.2 litre engine, and

had a Lotus Type number (81, shared with a GP car). It won the 1981 World Rally Championship for Makes. This association also led to Lotus development of the Chrysler 2.2 litre Turbo III engine.

● An agreement between Lotus and Toyota was announced in June 1982, as 'long term'; it led to the use of Toyota components in Lotus production cars.

● General Motors acquired a majority shareholding in Group Lotus plc as 1986 opened. Among developments, this led to Lotus taking over the Millbrook Proving Ground (until 1993); to interchange with Isuzu (for example, the new Elan used an Isuzu engine, while the handling and ride of the Isuzu Piazza was transformed by Lotus input, hence that car carried 'Handling by Lotus' badges); to Lotus Engineering design and development work on Chevrolet LT5 dohc 5.7 litre V8 for Corvette ZR1, and the high-performance version of Opel/Vauxhall Omega/Carlton (see page 68).

● Lotus undertook 'active suspension' work on the Alvis Scorpion armoured vehicle from 1992.

● Bugatti Industries acquired Group Lotus in August 1992, hence a Bugatti appeared on the Lotus stand at the 1994 British Motor Show, as Lotus entered into a short-lived commitment to distribute that car in the UK. Fortunately, the Bugatti controlling company was registered in Luxembourg, so the predictable failure of Bugatti Automobili did not drag Lotus down (in fact, Lotus contributed a healthy trading profit to the group in 1994).

formally set up in 1980). In 1981 only 345 cars were sold, and Grand Prix fortunes slumped.

As the De Lorean scandals loomed in the 1980s, there was a complex refinancing package, with David Wickens briefly taking the helm as Chairman. Alan Curtis took his place, until Group Lotus plc Chief Executive Mike Kimberley took on the role in 1991. There was some lack of continuity at management levels, and for the factory floor staff, too (Lotus had always been staunchly opposed to trade union activity and in the past its workers had been accustomed to switching from building customer racing cars to road cars as demand fluctuated, while in Spring 1992 all production was halted for five weeks, and little more than a year later the decision to end Elan production cost 300 jobs). On the plus side, Tony Rudd won for Lotus a commission to develop the V8 for GM's ZR1 Corvette.

Above: Colin Chapman in 1980.

The final days of the independent Team Lotus were sad, but irrelevant to the Group, and towards the mid-1990s there was a slow and successful growth in the Engineering involvement in GT racing. And there were the remarkable bicycles, the Lotus Sport carbon-composite machines that Chris Boardman rode to win an Olympic Gold Medal and break records captured headlines Lotus had not known since the heady Grand Prix days.

Another chapter opened in the Summer of 1993, when Bugatti Industries bought Lotus from General Motors, and Romano Artioli became Chairman. Apart from some Lotus technical input into Bugatti and a joint sales arrangement in the UK, the companies were kept apart. Within two years the collapse of Artioli's Bugatti companies encouraged speculation about another change of ownership. Managing Director Adrian Palmer gave

Above: The E-Auto concept shown in model form in 1993 envisaged a four-seat family car that could achieve 2.82 litres/100km (100mpg) at 120km/h (75mph).

Left: The Talbot Sunbeam-Lotus (Lotus 81) was a high-performance hatchback with a Lotus 2.2 litre engine, which sold in modest numbers. It was used by Talbot's rally team from 1978, winning the World Championship in 1981. This car, still largely in works team colours, was an independent entry in the 1983 Scottish Rally. This project was initiated under Chrysler control; other rally cars partly developed when Peugeot-Citroën took over the Talbot name were stillborn.

way to Rod Mansfield in 1995, but that appointment was short-lived – it seemed that Artioli was just not prepared to delegate real executive power.

In March 1995 Lotus completed its 50,000th car, an Elan S2. There was a touch of irony in that, for the rights had been passed to Kia, which launched the Elan in its home market at the start of 1996 as 'the first Korean sports car'!

Early in 1996, Lotus confirmed that major industrial concerns –not financial organizations –

had made offers 'to develop the business through cooperation for mutual benefit', implying that investment would be acceptable to strengthen the company. Artioli was obviously reluctant to sell the company, and during a turbulent period he sacked the board. To his credit, he also saw the Elise through to production.

Soon it was widely assumed that Daewoo would take over, while a British consortium or Samsung were also considered to be possible buyers. Daewoo's offer was on the table into the Autumn, when most industry observers regarded the Korean takeover as a deal done. But in the event, Perusahan Otomobil Nasional Berhard (Proton) acquired a controlling interest in Lotus from ACBN Holdings SA Luxembourg, the announcement coming after a brief flurry of rumours in October.

Romano Artioli retained a 20 per cent holding, and remained as a director of Lotus.

Immediately, Proton provided working capital. Proton undertook to provide 'manufacturing strengths' and resources: it was also suggested that it would increase Elise production to meet the strong demand, and that the car might be built in Malaya with a Proton engine.

Importantly, Lotus' R&D work was secure – contracts with General Motors were reckoned to provide almost two thirds of Lotus turnover, and this was vital to the car-building side. The Elise promised much, and in 1996 the long-awaited V8 – Lotus' first all-new engine since 1972 – had been introduced. Lotus' survival as a car manufacturer, which had sometimes seemed in doubt in the last quarter of the 20th century, seemed assured into the 21st century.

Above: The Lotus Sport time-trials bicycle with its distinctive all-carbon frame achieved instant Olympic Games fame in the hands of Chris Boardman in 1992.

15

LOTUS INNOVATIONS

This is a partial list, as some of Lotus' work for other companies has been confidential, and some of Chapman's own work, from his Vanwall Grand Prix car chassis/suspension development to the Resinject system, has also been omitted. Dates are approximate, as they normally refer to car introductions rather than the start of design.

● First production road car with glass fibre unitary chassis/body – Type 14 Elite, 1957

● 'Chapman strut' suspension – Type 12 F2 car, 1957

● First Grand Prix car with monocoque chassis – Type 25, 1962

● First road car to combine steel backbone chassis and glass-fibre body shell – Type 26 Elan, 1962

● First rear-engined Grand Prix car using engine as load-bearing chassis member – Type 49, 1967

● First Grand Prix car with gas turbine engine – Type 56B, 1970

● Grand Prix car with 'wedge' body lines – Type 72, 1972

● First 'ground effects' Grand Prix car – Type 78, 1977

● Vacuum Assisted Resin Injection (VARI) moulding process – Type 82 Esprit, 1987

● Active suspension: Esprit test vehicle, 1981; demonstrated, 1983; Type 92 F1 car conversion raced in 1983; two GP victories scored by 'active' 99T in 1987

● Tiny flat-twin, air-cooled engine for ultra-light aircraft shown at 1983 London Motorfair; this 480cc unit was abandoned when Colin Chapman died.

● Active noise cancellation, 1985

● Active rear-wheel steering, 1986

● 'Interactive wishbone' front suspension – Type 100 Elan, 1989

● Carbon-composite monocoque bicycle, 1992; Sport 110 bicycle, 1994

● Extruded aluminium suspension uprights, aluminium MMC brake discs (previously used only in racing), and epoxy-bonded extruded aluminium chassis – Type 111 Elise, 1995

Lotus Mk VI

THIS WAS the first true Lotus, in that it owed nothing to the Austin-Seven-based 1948-52 cars, and with 110 built it could almost be regarded as a 'production model' – the term is used cautiously as it was essentially a kit car. Confusingly, the first car designated Mk VI did follow on from earlier cars, as it was built for trials use; the regular Mk VI – eight were built early in 1953 – were basic dual-purpose cars, which could be used on the road, but are usually associated with club racing.

The Mk VI featured a multi-tubular space frame chassis that weighed a mere 25kg (55lb), with stressed aluminium panels forming the floor, scuttle and sides, and also increasing rigidity. The chassis was to be married to new or used Ford components by the buyer. The Ford Ten/Popular beam front

Below: The Mk VI appeared straightforward, but its basis was a sophisticated space frame, which was light and strong.

SPECIFICATION	LOTUS MK VI
ENGINE	4 cylinders, side valve, 1099cc
HORSEPOWER	31bhp @ 6000rpm (single carb) 40-45bhp (twin carb)
TRANSMISSION	Manual Ford 3-speed
CHASSIS	Space frame
SUSPENSION	Front independent, rear rigid axle
BRAKES	Drum
TOP SPEED*	120km/h (75mph) to 182km/h (113mph)
ACCELERATION	N/A

* With Ford engines, according to capacity and state of tune

axle was cut in half to make a swing axle front suspension, a Ford rigid axle was used at the rear, and there were prominent coil spring/damper units front and rear. The suspension was soft, and in the light Mk VI it combined with the rigid chassis to give tenacious roadholding, well in advance of contemporary small sports cars.

Owners were to install a variety of engines, but as Chapman intended, Ford units were most common, the Consul unit with its capacity fractionally reduced to bring it within the 1500cc category, or the 1172cc side-valve engine, in that capacity for 1172 Formula events or linered down to 1100cc for that sports car class. A Ford three-speed gearbox with Buckler close-ratio gears was normal.

The first cars started life with enclosed rear wheels, and skimpy front cycle wings were normal, although full 'touring' wings were suggested for road use, together with a full windscreen in place of the aero 'screen.

The first race for a Mk VI was at Silverstone

Above: Rear detail of Mk VI, chassis M6/51. Unusually – perhaps uniquely – it has a Ford engine with an Elva ohv conversion and twin SU carburettors (right).

in July 1952, and cars were run in competition long after Mk VI production had ended late in 1955. Lotus claimed that the four cars raced in 1953 won 19 races, and were also successful in sprints and hill climbs – and, of course, they were driven to venues. Mike Costin built the ninth Mk VI, which was successfully raced by Colin Chapman in his role as his company's works driver.

Lotus Seven

AN ENTHUSIAST'S no-frills sports car, this amazing little machine has had a very long life, prospering in the face of trends to 'civilize' the type. On one hand it has been a quite exceptional fun car – 'motorcycling on four wheels' is a common description – and on the other a serious competitions car.

It seemingly had low priority, for almost two years passed between the last Mk VI and the announcement of the Seven. As an aside, a one-off commissioned chassis was briefly referred to as the Mk VII in 1952, but this was completed as the Clairmonte and did not rate a Lotus type number.

The Seven announced in 1957 was the first of four series models to carry the Lotus badge; as it seemed an anachronism in the Lotus range, the rights were passed to Caterham Cars in 1973, and during the next two decades it was to be re-engineered from nose to tail, while the essential character was preserved.

Above: The 40bhp BMC engine of the Series 1 Seven shown below. The S1 cost £511 in kit form in 1959. The car shown here is owned by Caterham Cars.

Left: This 1965 Ford-Cosworth-powered Series 2 car is also part of the Caterham Collection.

The chassis followed the general lines of the Mk VI and was to be modified through the Seven's Lotus years, for example simplified in the 1960 S2 cars ('S' is standard Lotus shorthand for Series), then strengthened as a steel bulkhead and toe box became stressed members and the rear was beefed up in S3 cars (broadly, the version that became the Caterham Seven). The front suspension was by wishbones and coil spring/damper units; at the rear there was a live axle, from the Standard Ten or Austin Metropolitan at first and later from the Ford Escort, located by radius arms, with coil springs/damper units. Front disc brakes came with the Super Seven in 1962.

The simplest and cheapest cars had Ford 1172cc side-valve engines and three-speed gearboxes; the first Super Seven had a Coventry Climax 1097cc FWA engine and four-speed BMC gearbox, as well

as the distinguishing feature of wire wheels. In S2/S3 days most cars had Ford or modified Ford engines, and Ford all-synchromesh 'boxes. The ultimate Lotus Seven was the S3 Twin Cam SS, with a Lotus Twin Cam or 1.6 litre Holbay-tuned Ford

SPECIFICATION	LOTUS SEVEN S1
ENGINE*	4 cylinders, side valve, 1172cc
HORSEPOWER	40bhp @ 4500rpm
TRANSMISSION	Manual Ford 3-/4-speed
CHASSIS	Space frame
SUSPENSION	Front independent, rear live axle
BRAKES	Drum
TOP SPEED	130km/h (81mph)
ACCELERATION	0-96km/h (60mph): 16.2 seconds

* Alternative power units included BMC 948cc pushrod ohv engine and Coventry Climax 1097cc FWA

dohc engine providing 125bhp to propel its 571kg (1258lb) – brick-like aerodynamic qualities limited the top speed to just over 161km/h (100mph), but in 0-60mph (virtually 0-100km/h) timing it would out-accelerate a Jaguar E-Type. This performance called for 'reinstatement' of the S1 engine bay and cockpit triangulation in the frame . . .

SPECIFICATION	LOTUS S2 SUPER SEVEN
ENGINE	4 cylinders, pushrod ohv, 1340cc
HORSEPOWER	85bhp @ 6000rpm
TRANSMISSION	Manual Ford 4-speed
CHASSIS	Space frame
SUSPENSION	Front independent, rear live axle
BRAKES	Drum
TOP SPEED	163km/h (102mph)
ACCELERATION	0-96km/h (60mph): 7.7 seconds

19

Caterham's immaculate 1965 car (below) has the long flowing front wings usually associated with the Seven. The Ford-based power unit fills the engine bay (left), while the external spare wheel mounting is in a 1930s' sports car tradition (right); the niggardly boot was useful for little more than stowing the soft top and side screens. The cockpit (opposite) was cramped and an 'elbow-out' driving position became natural (so did 'Lotus elbow'!). The wood-rimmed steering wheel is typical of the period. Rev counter, oil pressure gauge and water temperature gauges face the driver, an ammeter and speedo face the passenger.

20

22

Primary functions had absolute priority, and cockpit comfort was not among them, especially for drivers of above-average height or girth (Caterham introduced a long-cockpit Seven in 1981). The seat cushion was on the floor, the back rested against the rear panel. Access for a person designed to fit the car was simple, and the essentials 'fell to hand', save the awkward hand-brake lever. In the low-price versions only essentials were provided – soft top and windscreen wiper were extras – and there was no fuel gauge until the S3 in 1968.

The S2 Seven America had carpets, so did S3 cars. The Super Seven could have a heater. S2 cars had better instruments, soft top and side screens,

and the long flared wings that came during this series were sometimes retro-fitted to S1 cars (parts interchange can confuse identification).

The styling of the S4 introduced by Lotus in 1970 is generally considered retrograde. The chassis relied more on steel panels for strength (it was less rigid), and it carried an unstressed moulded glass-fibre body, designed by Alan Barrett. The main front part carried separate but well-integrated wings. There was even a little luggage compartment, albeit really no more useful than the niggardly well above the battery and fuel tank in the earlier cars, and the soft top was certainly better (a hardtop alternative was shown, although not listed). Three

Above: The Seven Series 3 Twin Cam was a fierce little car, with a 125 bhp Lotus-Holbay engine. This car, TC/1, was shown at the 1969 London Motor Show, and is now owned by Graham Nearn.

engine alternatives were suggested, to drive through a Ford Corsair gearbox.

The cockpit was still tight, entry still difficult and not elegant, there was still no stowage space for odds and ends, but at least the seats were padded and more supportive.

A new Type number, 60, emphasized that this was a different car, and as Lotus Components sought to widen the market for its little sports car, it also reflected a need to restrain costs. It succeeded, in that some 900 were sold in three years, out of a total of 2,477 Lotus-originated Sevens (that official total could be too precise, as many were kits). The S4 was profitable, but the last was built in October 1972.

Caterham took over the S4, but soon abandoned it as parts stocks ran down, and Graham Nearn recognized that the timeless image of the less comfortable earlier models was still attractive – and he was proved so right, on and on towards the end of the century. In some ways, the Europa was regarded as a successor, but the next Lotus to embody the same spirit did not come until 1995, when the Elise was announced . . .

Above The lines of the Seven S4 were not admired (this was the last Seven built by Lotus). Ford engine (left) was normal.

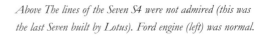

SPECIFICATION	LOTUS SEVEN S4
ENGINE*	4 cylinders, pushrod ohv, 1599cc
HORSEPOWER	84bhp @ 5500rpm
TRANSMISSION	Manual Ford 4-speed
CHASSIS	Space frame
SUSPENSION	Front independent, rear live axle
BRAKES	Disc front, drum rear
TOP SPEED	161km/h (100mph)
ACCELERATION	0-96km/h (60mph): 8.8 seconds

* Alternative power units were the Ford 1300cc Kent engine and the Lotus Twin Cam engine

Lotus Eleven

THE aerodynamic front-engined sports cars of the 1950s were essentially circuit cars, but they could be used on public roads, and the Eleven Sports was introduced as an adequately equipped road car, while leading magazines completed road tests of 'racing' Elevens. This name was always spelled out; it marked the end of Lotus' Roman numeral designations, and was followed by the first in the Type sequence.

The first of the slippery little sports-racers was the VIII of 1954, with a full-width body designed by aerodynamicist Frank Costin. The 1955 IX was more compact, and had more prominent tail fins, to improve cross winds stability with such a light car. The Club had 1172cc Ford or 1098cc Climax engines, and a Ford live rear axle, while the Le Mans had a de Dion rear end, disc brakes and bigger engines. The X was similar, with 2-litre engines.

Like its forerunners, the Eleven was built around a space frame. It overshadowed them, in appearance, its competitions record, and production numbers. Some 250 were built, 1956-58, in three basic versions: Le Mans (Coventry Climax FWA or FWB engines), Club (Climax engine) and Sports, with Ford engines and intended for road use. Several other types of engine were to be fitted. The S2 cars came in 1957 with wishbone and coil spring independent front suspension and tougher rear axles.

All had Costin's beautiful thigh-high body, this time fully equipped with lights. The nose was front-hinged, giving generous access to the engine; the tail was rear-hinged, covering space for battery, spare wheel and minimal luggage (a little more could be squeezed into side pockets).

The wrap-round Perspex windscreen, so low that a tall driver would normally look over it, merged into side sections incorporated in little bottom-hinged doors. Fore-and-aft seat room was reasonable, but cockpit width was restricted. Circuit cars tended to have fairings over the passenger space and a headrest merging into a large fin. Independent bodies ranged from a practical open two-seater by coachbuilder Ghia to a 'gullwing' coupé by Frank Costin. Intended for circuit use, this retained the original body back to the scuttle, but was transformed with a fastback GT cockpit and tail, and less obviously a full undershield (in the mid-1970s it was rescued by Rod Leach and restored by Lynx).

The Eleven was responsive, and a little 'nervous'. It weighed some 500kg (1100lb) unladen and drag was low, so the 1100 Climax engine in 84bhp form propelled a late Le Mans to 200km/h

Left: Startline marshals at Goodwood give scale to this Lotus Eleven – it was a very low car, small and with attractive, slippery lines.

SPECIFICATION	LOTUS ELEVEN S1 LE MANS
ENGINE	FWA – 4 cylinders, sohc, 1098cc
HORSEPOWER	83bhp @ 6800rpm
TRANSMISSION	Manual 4-speed
CHASSIS	Space frame
SUSPENSION	Front independent, rear de Dion
BRAKES	Disc
TOP SPEED	193km/h (120mph)
ACCELERATION	0-96km/h (60mph): 10.2 seconds

(125mph), and gave a 0-80km/h (0-50mph) time of 8 seconds.

Elevens dominated small-car race classes in the second half of the 1950s, with considerable success at Le Mans in 1956-57. The 15, a development intended for larger engines, and the 17 designed on similar lines, failed to match the record of the Eleven, a sports car classic by any 1950s or 1990s standards.

Right: Climax engines were normal in circuit Elevens.
Below: Costin's one-off coupé body was not for tall drivers!

SPECIFICATION	LOTUS ELEVEN S2 LE MANS 85
ENGINE	Stage 2 FWA – 4 cylinders, sohc, 1098cc
HORSEPOWER	84bhp @ 6800rpm
TRANSMISSION	Manual 4-speed
CHASSIS	Space frame
SUSPENSION	Front independent, rear de Dion
BRAKES	Disc
TOP SPEED	200km/h (125mph)
ACCELERATION	0-96km/h (60mph): 10 seconds

Lotus Elite

THE ELITE – Lotus 14 – was launched at the same time as the Seven, but was in complete contrast. It was the first closed Lotus road car; it was sleek; its performance was outstanding. In technical respects it was a landmark car, and it also pointed towards Lotus becoming a serious production car company. However, the concept may have been too ambitious for the infant company, which could ill afford the money it apparently lost on every sale, or the Elite's reputation for poor reliability – it was fragile, bits did fall off, and there were too many problem areas for unsympathetic service mechanics.

The prototype that was shown at the 1957 London Motor Show was incomplete, lacking components such as radiator and prop shaft. The first customer cars were delivered at the end of 1958, and serious production did not get under way before the second anniversary of its announcement.

Lotus simply did not have the resources to undertake traditional production tooling, and the Elite had a glass-fibre unitary chassis/body (in the little Berkeley that appeared on similar lines a year earlier, the stressed moulded underframe had alloy pressings to ensure rigidity). The three main Elite sections comprised the floor pan, incorporating a

Below: The moulded monocoque of the Elite was a world first, and outwardly its coupé lines are timeless.

SPECIFICATION	LOTUS ELITE S1
ENGINE	4 cylinders, sohc, 1216cc
HORSEPOWER	75bhp @ 6100rpm (single carb) 83bhp @ 6300rpm (twin carb)
TRANSMISSION	Manual 4-speed
CHASSIS	Glass-fibre monocoque
SUSPENSION	Independent front and rear
BRAKES	Disc
TOP SPEED	183km/h (114mph) – single carb 191km/h (119mph) – twin carb
ACCELERATION	0-96km/h (60mph): 11.4 seconds (single carb engine)

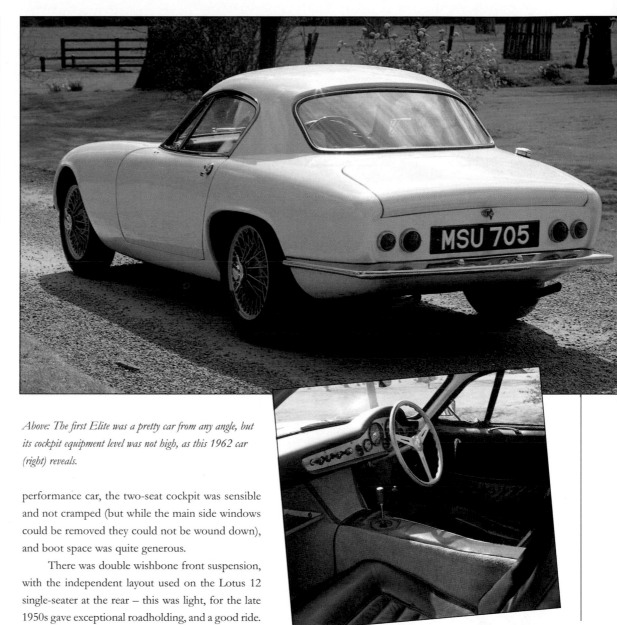

Above: The first Elite was a pretty car from any angle, but its cockpit equipment level was not high, as this 1962 car (right) reveals.

small metal sub-frame for the front suspension and with a flat undertray that contributed to aerodynamic efficiency; a longitudinal centre section (engine bay, transmission tunnel, wheel arches and boot); and the coupé body. A steel hoop bonded around the windscreen increased rigidity and provided door hinge mountings. Mechanical components were bolted through the glass fibre, with metal inserts at mounting points, and rubber protection where metal parts might chafe. Most body shells were made by Bristol Aircraft.

The chassis was very rigid, but interior noise levels could be high (sparse cockpit furnishing did little to help here!). Peter Kirwan-Taylor, who had proposed a coupé Eleven and was one of the instigators of the project, styled the body, which was refined by John Frayling with some input by Frank Costin. There was only a little wind-tunnel work with models, but the estimated drag coefficient of 0.29 has seldom been matched. Elegance was combined with practicality – getting in was not a problem with this low high-performance car, the two-seat cockpit was sensible and not cramped (but while the main side windows could be removed they could not be wound down), and boot space was quite generous.

There was double wishbone front suspension, with the independent layout used on the Lotus 12 single-seater at the rear – this was light, for the late 1950s gave exceptional roadholding, and a good ride.

Left: The Elite was a highly successful GT racing car. This is one of the Team Elite cars prominent in 1961–63.

Above: An Elite being put through its paces in front of a crowded Silverstone stand.

The variations are probably due to spare shells which were built up later.

GT racing was in Chapman's mind when the Elite was laid down, and on circuits it excelled. Pre-production cars completed at the Edmonton workshops, where the prototype was built, were loaned to racing teams in 1958 (that made for low-cost development mileage, too!), and from 1959 the Elite made an impression at international level, first with a class win in the Nürburgring 1000km race. Elites won their class at Le Mans five times from 1959, were twice 8th overall, and won the prestigious Index of Thermal Efficiency in 1960 and 1962. In 1962, Hobbs and Gardner covered 3,847km (2,390 miles) at 160.29km/h (99.6mph) on their way to 8th overall – a distance first achieved by an outright winner only ten years earlier! Elites were prominent in British and North American national racing through to the mid-1960s, when Elans largely supplanted them.

The Coventry Climax engine was an all-alloy unit, conceived for fire-pump use with allowance for free internal oil flow, hence the Elite's reputation as an 'oil-burner'. This FWE was light, and substitute engines upset the balance of the Elite. Twin-carb engines were optional on S2 cars, and the Special Equipment (SE) version of 1962 had an 85bhp FWE; the 23 Super 95 cars, and six Super 100 and six Super 105 Elites had designations suggesting power outputs. Years later, a Lotus Twin Cam was tried in a spare chassis, while Climax engines from 742cc to 2 litres were used in racing Elites. BMC gearboxes were normal at first, with ZF close-ratio 'boxes available in the SE, and the efficacy of a Hobbs automatic transmission was demonstrated in racing.

This brave design, with its timeless styling, deserves its high status among automotive 'classics'. But in its time, the Elite was not a great success. Measured performance with a small engine may have been excellent, but some customers may have wanted more for the price – an Elite was expensive, and sales never reached a viable level. The collapse of Lotus' US distributor in 1960 was a contributory problem.

In Britain, the Elite was offered in component form from 1961, and this moved some stock (the cost was cut by more than a third, and assembly was reckoned to take 25 hours). Production ended in Autumn 1963, when 1078 had been built – that was Lotus' figure in the 1990s, it had earlier quoted 990, and figures between the two have been published.

Above: Mike Parkes, pictured here, three-wheeling an Elite in the 1960 TT.

Lotus Elan

FOR MANY enthusiasts, the Elan was the outstanding small sports car of the 1960s – pretty and practical, civilized and comfortable, efficient and quick, in any of its forms. The novel construction of the Elite was largely expedient, the pioneering chassis of the Type 26 Elan was sound automotive engineering. The car was a commercial success, too – the first Lotus to achieve five-figure production.

Thoughts about another glass-fibre chassis were set aside, and the Elan was built around a fabricated steel backbone, forked front and rear to the suspension mountings, with engine and gearbox between the 'prongs' of the front fork and transmission running along the boxed backbone. The chassis was light and stiff, but vulnerable to corrosion. The suspension comprised coil springs and wishbones deriving from the Triumph Herald at

the front, Chapman struts and lower wishbones at the rear. It was soft, and generally made for sure-footed, neutral, and predictable handling; with skinny tyres there were shortcomings on wet roads. Ride qualities were excellent.

The glass-fibre body was largely attributed to Ron Hickman, and was made by Lotus. It was lightly stressed, and offered little protection in a side impact accident. Launch cars were open, a hard top came within months (in May 1963) and a coupé was

Below: This is believed to be the first production Elan (26/0017), sold by Lotus in January 1963.

SPECIFICATION	LOTUS ELAN S1 and S2
ENGINE	4 cylinders, dohc, 1498cc (later 1558cc)
HORSEPOWER	100bhp @ 5700rpm (later 105bhp @ 5500rpm)
TRANSMISSION	Manual 4-speed
CHASSIS	Backbone
SUSPENSION	Independent front and rear
BRAKES	Disc
TOP SPEED	185km/h (115mph) (1.6 litre)
ACCELERATION	0-96km/h (60mph): 9 sec (1.6 litre)

Above: The cockpit layout of the S1 Elan was straightforward. Right: The Twin Cam engine.

introduced with the S3 Elan in 1965. In 1963, incidentally, a Lotus press release proudly announced the 1000th Elan – 'it took more than twice as long to produce 1000 Elites'.

The Lotus Twin Cam engine was first seen in the 23 sports-racing car in 1962, but was always intended for the Elan. Broadly, it comprised the block of the Ford 116E pushrod ohv engine with an aluminium twin-cam head designed by Harry Mundy. In the first Elans it was a 1498cc 100bhp unit, but this soon gave way to the 1558cc version, rated at 105bhp in 1963. In this 'blue cam cover' form it was flexible and pulled strongly through its effective revs range (it was easy to over-rev, so there was a 6500rpm ignition cut out). There were to be variations, notably in carburettors.

The kerb weight of the Elan was 688kg (1516lb) and 105bhp gave it an impressive top speed of 185km/h (115mph) with 100mph (say 160km/h) reached from rest in 26.8 seconds. It matched the Elite in its modest fuel demands.

The transmission incorporated the excellent Ford four-speed gearbox, and a shortcoming that was to become familiar – rubber 'doughnuts', the Metalastik couplings in the drive shafts intended to iron out shocks, which wound up and led to surging.

Despite the narrow seats, cockpit space was good, and so was luggage space. Cockpit trim was hardly luxurious and some details were poor, save on a few cars with coachbuilt interiors.

A competitions version of this Lotus was not inevitable. Rather than see normal Elans raced, Chapman introduced the 26R, with lighter bodywork, fixed headlights faired into the wings in place of the pop-up items, modified suspension and engines giving up to 140bhp in 1964, with a claimed 158bhp in the later BRM-developed Twin Cam. The 26R accounted for 97 of the 2150 S1/S2 Elans built, and it became prominent in national and club racing. Ian Walker Racing built a pretty fastback one-off, but this was destroyed in its second race.

The Elan was fractionally larger than the early Austin-Healey Sprite, which Chapman might have had in mind when he conceived it (in performance it was of course in another class altogether). The S3 and S4 cars showed a clear evolutionary trend away from 'sports' towards 'GT'.

The S3 fixed-head coupé (Type 36) came in Autumn 1965, an SE version early in 1966 with detail enhancements from centre-lock wheels to fitted carpets. The 115bhp rating for the engine might have been optimistic, but it gave a 198km/h (123mph) top speed. These improvements featured on the S3 convertible (Type 45) later in 1966. The S4 fixed head and drophead models that came in 1968 were outwardly distinguished by low profile tyres. There was much more to identify the +2 (Type 50) that had been introduced six months earlier, anticipated to a degree by a Frua 2+2 fastback body on an Elan, shown in 1964.

Below: An Elan S4 in the colours of Team Lotus sponsors, with a modest bonnet bulge and flared wheel arches.

different, both overall and in details such as the combined side lights/indicators in the front wings, outboard of the main pop-up lights. The cockpit was better equipped and finished, and modest through-flow ventilation was provided.

Despite greater weight and a firmer ride, the +2 was still a sensitive car. Infuriatingly the drive-shaft wind-up problem remained. Aerodynamics were slightly better (estimated drag was 0.30) and with the SE engine rated at 118bhp, it was still quick, with 190km/h (118mph) possible. Acceleration did not match the two-seater Elans, but was still brisk (0-100mph, or roughly 0-160km/h), in 25.8 seconds. The 1969 +2S was refined in detail, especially in better cockpit furnishing. This was the first Lotus road car not offered in component ('kit') form.

SPECIFICATION	LOTUS ELAN S4 SPRINT
ENGINE	4 cylinders, dohc, 1558cc
HORSEPOWER	126bhp @ 6500rpm
TRANSMISSION	Manual 4-speed (late cars, 5-speed optional)
CHASSIS	Backbone
SUSPENSION	Independent front and rear
BRAKES	Disc
TOP SPEED	193km/h (120mph)
ACCELERATION	0-96km/h (60mph): 7 seconds

Left: The open Elans were most attractive cars viewed from any angle. This 1968 S3 convertible has the door window frames that had been used on the fixed-head coupé.
Below: This Special Equipment Elan is identified by details such as the indicator repeaters above the front wheels and the SE badges just behind them. It was completed a little later than the red car.

A new name would have been justified – there had been a proposal to call it Elite 2, and the Elan name was to be dropped later in 1968. Two small rear seats were the qualification for the description, but these were more suitable for luggage than children over a journey of any distance. It was 580mm (23in) longer than the S4, and 190mm (7.5in) wider, while kerb weight was up to 878kg (1934lb). Market assessments suggested that an open version was not worthwhile, but some specialists undertook the re-engineering independently. Lotus also toyed with a project that envisaged interchangeable bodywork behind the B pillar.

The 2+2 was more than a stretched Elan. The sleek one-piece moulded body was obviously

As Elan sales dipped, an early task for Tony Rudd was the development of the 'big valve' engine. Its familiar nickname derived from the main improvement, which was coupled with an increased compression ratio and a reversion to twin Weber carburettors (Strombergs had been used, to meet US emissions regulations). It was rated at 126bhp, and that led Lotus to strengthen the drive line, which in turn meant that stouter universal joints were used . . . and those surge characteristics were at last eliminated.

It was introduced in the Elan S4 Sprint and the +2S 130 in 1971, and on the last cars drove through a five-speed gearbox, anticipating its use in the next Lotus generation. The Sprint had a two-tone 'Gold Leaf' colour. scheme and slightly extended wheel arches. It is generally recognized as the most desirable first-generation Elan, faster than sports car contemporaries with larger engines, a top speed of 193km/h (120mph), and handling that was still a class above its rivals.

Sprint production ended in February 1973, but the +2S outlived it by almost two years. The optional five-speed gearbox was particularly appropriate in this GT car (when fitted, from late 1972, it became the +2S 130/5). It was capable of matching the Sprint's top speed, and as fifth was an overdrive gear, high cruising speeds could be maintained at economical engine revs. Incidentally, odd late Elans were converted with estate car bodies, while some were finished in Team Lotus black and gold colours. This last model in the first Elan line was discontinued at the end of 1974, when 5168 had been built, to be added to the 12,224 cars that actually carried the Elan name. Thus it was the most successful Lotus during Chapman's years . . .

Below: The greater length of the Elan +2S is obvious in this 1974 car; the pale colour shows its lines to advantage.

SPECIFICATION	LOTUS ELAN +2 SE
ENGINE	4 cylinders, dohc, 1558cc
HORSEPOWER	118bhp @ 6000rpm
TRANSMISSION	Manual 4-speed
CHASSIS	Backbone
SUSPENSION	Independent front and rear
BRAKES	Disc
TOP SPEED	190km/h (118mph)
ACCELERATION	0-96km/h (60mph): 9.6 seconds

Above: The Elan S4 Sprint was originally seen in two-tone Gold Leaf Team Lotus colours, which seemed to suit it better than the overall blue of this car. Distinctive styling details such as the extended wheel arches and centre-lock wheels give it a more purposeful appearance, while the through-flow air vents point to greater sophistication for this desirable model. Right: The 26R was the competitions version of the Elan, substantially modified and distinguished by details such as headlights faired into the wings. This 26R is running in the 1966 Spa 1000km race.

Lotus-Cortina

SALOONS may seem out of place here, but the first to carry the Lotus name, and its type number, 28, was important to the health of the company in the 1960s. Ford's Walter Hayes saw Lotus' Twin Cam engine as the ideal unit for a high-performance version of the Cortina – worldwide Ford was setting out in pursuit of a 'Total Performance' image – and took the initiative in the project. The car was announced within three months of the Elan, in January 1963, and it ran in parallel with it.

In road form, the engine was rated at 105bhp and there was a 145bhp 'racing' version; at the time, the normal Cortina 1.5 litre engine gave 59.5bhp.

The transmission, notably the excellent four-speed gearbox, comprised modified Cortina components.

Chapman was allowed to undertake more than an engine substitution, but the basic lines of the two-door body were unchanged. The Twin Cam was heavier than the standard engine, so until 1964 the bare body shells that were delivered to Cheshunt were fitted with rather fragile aluminium doors, bonnet and boot lid.

Those early cars also had Chapman's ingenious rear suspension, with coil spring/damper units replacing the half-elliptic springs, trailing radius arms and a central A-frame for lateral location. This proved fragile – rear-seat passengers and a luggage load were discouraged – and it had a tendency to cause oil leaks in the differential casing. From June 1965 the normal Cortina GT rear suspension was used, with an incidental advantage in noise reduction. It was also more robust, and that was welcomed by the Ford rally team.

Mk 1 production meant that the model was homologated for 'Group 2' saloon racing, and Lotus Components built almost a hundred rather special racing Lotus-Cortinas. These gained many race victories in Europe and beyond. Sir John Whitmore won the European Touring Car Championship in 1965, driving an Alan Mann team car with BRM-prepared 150bhp engine, and spectators enjoyed a lot of spectacular three-wheel cornering by leading drivers, notably Jim Clark.

Left: In the mid-1960s saloon racing Lotus-Cortinas dominated the 2-litre class, and made life difficult for large-car drivers. Here the works cars, Pete Arundell leading, sandwich Baillie's Ford Falcon at Silverstone in 1966.

SPECIFICATION	LOTUS-CORTINA MK 1
ENGINE	4 cylinders, dohc, 1558cc
HORSEPOWER	105bhp @ 5500rpm
TRANSMISSION	Manual 4-speed
CHASSIS	Integral
SUSPENSION	Front independent, rear live axle
BRAKES	Disc front, drum rear
TOP SPEED	172km/h (107mph)
ACCELERATION	0-96km/h (60mph): 9.9 seconds

Right: The works pair at Crystal Palace, Arundell ahead of Ickx in 73, about to take on Falcons and Mustangs. Below: Rally success came in Canada, when Roger Clark (on bonnet) won the 1966 Shell 4000.

The early version was not a wholly practical road car, but there was a facelift early in 1964 and some refinements were carried over from main-line Cortinas. The first Lotus-Cortina was discontinued in Summer, 1966, when 3301 had been built.

Lotus had no production involvement in the Mk 2 that was announced early in 1967; this did not have a Lotus type number and soon lost its Lotus badges. The engine was a little more powerful, but the car was heavier and closer to other Cortinas, in two- and four-door forms with the full range of body colours listed. Some were used in competition (briefly raced by Team Lotus), but the true role of the Mk 2 was as a quick, comfortable and civilized road car. Production reached 4032.

37

Below and opposite below: An immaculate 1965 Lotus-Cortina, enhanced with non-standard road wheels, quite in the spirit of the car, as a wide range of special parts was listed by Ford in the interests of competition activities. The 1963-64 cockpit (right) was a straightforward arrangement, with an alloy-spoked wheel and 'satin-finished' fascia (the rev counter was red-lined at 6500rpm and the speedometer flanked by fuel and temperature gauges). Opposite: Revisions came late in 1964 as 'Aeroflow' cockpit ventilation was introduced. The engine, Lotus' twin-cam adaptation of the Ford Kent unit, normally had an ignition cut-out to guard against over-revving.

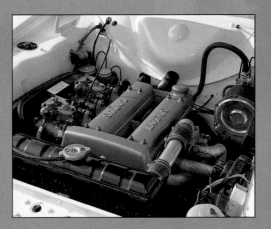

Lotus Europa

WHEN THE Europa was launched at the end of 1966, it was expected to become the successor to the seemingly outmoded Seven. It never did, and in its first version was rated interesting but flawed. Later it was taken more seriously.

In the Autumn of 1964 Chapman saw in the new front-wheel-drive Renault 16 saloon an engine/transmission unit that could be adapted for the mid-engined GT car he sought to introduce below the Elan in the Lotus range. The possibility of collaboration with another major European manufacturer was attractive, too (and perhaps equally to Régie Renault, despite its association with Alpine – after all, Lotus was a world championship Formula 1 constructor).

An agreement came quickly, and the new design, Type 46, was developed in 18 months; it was the first model to be built from inception at the new Hethel plant. At the time it was unusual, for only Lamborghini and Matra had mid-engined road cars in production, although rear-engined models (for example, Alpines and Porsches) were not uncommon.

The Type 46 was proclaimed as the 'Lotus for Europe', hence Europa, and the first two years' output was destined for mainland Europe, and from 1968 for the USA. Unit costs that would have enabled Lotus to market it in the British sector which Chapman aspired to were never achieved, despite a very favourable Renault deal, and a realistic UK price would have been uncomfortably close to that of the Elans.

The fabricated sheet-steel backbone chassis had the engine/transmission unit in a broad 'Y' at the rear, with a straight cross member at the front. The engine was a free-revving aluminium unit, mildly tuned for Lotus use. For European cars it was in 1470cc form, initially rated at 78bhp; cars destined for the USA had engines with increased bore and stroke, giving 1565cc, to offset the effects of emissions equipment. The 80bhp 'US' rating was soon surpassed by 'European' cars, with 82bhp. In

Left: The early Europa with high sides to the engine deck was distinctive from this angle, but far from handsome.

SPECIFICATION	LOTUS EUROPA S1
ENGINE	4 cylinders, pushrod ohv, 1470cc
HORSEPOWER	78bhp @ 6000rpm (later 82bhp)
TRANSMISSION	Manual 4-speed
CHASSIS	Backbone
SUSPENSION	Independent front and rear
BRAKES	Disc front, drum rear
TOP SPEED	177km/h (110mph)
ACCELERATION	0-96km/h (60mph): 9.5 seconds

SPECIFICATION	LOTUS EUROPA SPECIAL
ENGINE	4 cylinders, dohc, 1558cc
HORSEPOWER	126bhp @ 6500rpm
TRANSMISSION	Manual 4- or 5-speed
CHASSIS	Backbone
SUSPENSION	Independent front and rear
BRAKES	Disc front, drum rear
TOP SPEED	195km/h (121mph)
ACCELERATION	0-96km/h (60mph): 6.6 seconds

The moulded glass-fibre body was bonded to the chassis to increase rigidity (it also complicated repair and renovation work). The nose was clean, with radiator air taken in through the cut-out where the number plate had been on the Ford Anglia that contributed the bumper (the rear bumper came from the Ford Cortina). The Mini provided the headlights, which were fixed on this model. Behind the cockpit a flat engine deck was flanked by prominent buttresses; engine air was taken in through the wheel arches.

The cockpit was cramped, with fixed seats and adjustable controls. While the view ahead was excellent, rearward visibility was poor, and the single-pane door windows were fixed, in a petty contribution to cost reduction. Many later mid-engined cars had less luggage space, although the Europa's front and rear compartments were only really useable for modest amounts of soft baggage.

effect, the Renault engine/gearbox was turned through 180 degrees, so that the transmission was behind the engine. Little conversion work was needed, and it was carried out by Renault before the units were delivered to Lotus.

At the front, Triumph components were again used in the suspension, while the rear suspension comprised long box-section radius arms, lower links and fixed-length drive shafts, with coil springs/dampers.

The mechanical layout lent itself to a low body, and while the lines by stylist John Frayling were not universally admired, they were effective, with a 0.32 drag coefficient (Lotus claimed that the addition of a small rear spoiler after quarter-scale wind-tunnel tests gave an improvement from 0.34).

Left: The Type 47 racing derivative of the Europa shows off attractive nose lines, the wider centre-lock wheels, and fuel filler and flush intake behind the door.

Alongside the Elan, the Europa was lower – height 1079mm (42.5in) – but wider and longer. It was also lighter, at 612kg (1350lb). Critics gave it a lower rating than the Elan, in respects from measured performance to the gearshift and the sheer silly inconvenience of those fixed windows. Only in handling and roadholding was it considered superior.

The Lotus 47 derivative for circuit use was another matter. It came late in 1966, with the right-hand drive not offered on S1 Europas. Rear suspension was revised, and there were disc brakes all round, and late 47s (47A) had beefed-up chassis with a separate body shell. The major change was in the engine, with the Lotus Twin Cam in fuel-injection form giving double the power of the Renault unit (it drove through a Hewland five-speed gearbox, too).

The 'official' production figure was 55 cars, when the racing homologation requirement was 50 units (a few road 47Fs were built with 1.6 litre Ford Cortina engines, perhaps to make up the homologation numbers). The 47s performed well in secondary races, but proved fragile in longer events. The Lotus team then switched to the 62, which was outwardly similar, but was a very different machine, built around a space frame.

A one-off 47D was built for GKN/ Vandervell as a test bed, with a lengthened chassis and Rover 3.5 litre V8 driving through a ZF five-speed gearbox. Its top speed has been variously quoted, but 262km/h (163mph) was reliably measured (putting the 47D in the modern supercar class) while the 0-100mph (0-161km/h) acceleration figure was 11.1 seconds.

The S2 came in 1968, and in 1969 the Europa was launched on the British market, first complete and then in component form in 1970 ('kit' Europas

Below: The Europa Twin Cam was always highly regarded, especially this 1973 Europa Special variant with the 'big valve' engine.

were to be listed until early 1973). In the S2, the body was conventionally mounted to the chassis – this eased repairs and reduced cockpit noise – the side windows were divided vertically and the main ones could be opened (electrically), the seats were adjustable and cockpit fittings were improved. The Renault-engined S2 was discontinued in Autumn 1971, when just over 400 had been built, and independent engine conversions had underlined the need for a more potent version.

Autumn 1971 saw the introduction of the Lotus 74, the Europa Twin Cam. This was slightly longer to accommodate the Twin Cam engine; there was a small spoiler under the nose; the rear buttresses were discarded to give an overall flat deck. The engine was in 105bhp tune, 8 per cent larger than the 16 engine and giving 37 per cent more power. It lifted top speed to 188km/h (117mph), with 160km/h (100mph) cruising quite feasible. By no means incidentally, there was a little more room for a tall driver.

This model gave way to the Europa Special after a year. The Special had the 'big valve' engine developing 126bhp, and a five-speed gearbox was optional (standard for the last 18 months of production). In its last two years, the Europa at last had acceleration and speed to match its other virtues. And cockpit fittings were uprated again in late Summer 1973, moving the Europa still further from the original cheap sports car concept.

Production ended in September 1974, when 9887 had been built, just over 4000 of them with Renault engines, so in numerical terms the Europa was second only to the contemporary Elan in Lotus' first four decades.

Above: Many Europa Specials were painted in the familiar black and gold JPS colours worn by Team Lotus cars in the 1970s. There was no sign of the vestigial buttresses that did so little to enhance the rear quarters of the early Europa. In its 'big valve' form the engine (right) was rated at 126bhp and the car had a top speed of 195km/h (121mph).

Lotus Elite

THE ELITE name was revived for the Type 75, and this car marked a major change in Lotus' policy. During its six-year gestation Chapman saw it as an entry into the luxury GT sector, as a competitor for manufacturers such as Aston Martin. There were studies in the late 1960s; actual design work started early in 1971, and a prototype ran in January 1972.. The subsequent development phase was long, and Chapman was reported to be exasperated by this, the more so as he was excited by the M70 project that was to become the Esprit. Racing history shows that he should have been devoting more time to a GP car to replace the 72.

Eventually, Project M50 became Type 75, and was announced as the Elite in May 1974. The timing turned out to be fortunate in one respect – the car appeared during a major oil crisis, and its small engine deflected possible adverse reactions to a new GT car with 'executive' credentials.

The backbone chassis was retained, stronger and with a substantial cross member to take the two front engine mounts (the third was beneath the gearbox). In late production cars the backbone was galvanized. The independent suspension followed established Lotus lines, and as before, the rear brakes were mounted inboard.

The engine was Lotus' 907, an all-alloy, 16-valve, twin-cam unit. As the Elite programme ran late, this had been made available for the ill-starred Jensen-Healey sports car, where some teething problems were ironed out. Some shortcomings still showed in the Elite, for example 'four-cylinder ailments' such as vibration and some noise. As the car was announced, the 1973cc unit was rated at 155bhp, but that was soon increased to 160bhp (the Federal version with Zenith-Strombergs instead of two Dell 'Orto carburettors produced 140bhp, and met emissions requirements). It was canted at 45 degrees, and although the engine compartment seemed full, it was reasonably accessible (that did not mean that it was a machine for amateur maintenance). Lotus encouraged assessments that the introduction of this engine in a Lotus production car marked the company's emergence as a fully-fledged manufacturer.

The Elite had a five-speed gearbox, incorporating Austin Maxi gears in a Lotus casing, and fifth was an overdrive gear. A version with the Borg-Warner Model 65 three-speed automatic transmission was announced in 1975, although it was not available until early 1976.

The glass-fibre body was moulded in upper and lower parts, marked by the prominent longitudinal centre line in the styling, with a central part incorporating the front bulkhead. Chapman's patented Resinject system (injection moulding in place of the laying-up technique) was used. The wide doors had substantial built-in steel beams, which met side-intrusion requirements, provided stiffening and carried the window frame, hinges and lock. The integrity of the basic method of

Left: Pragmatism led to some compromises in the lines of the front-engined, four-seater Elite. Nevertheless, in side elevation it was a balanced design (opposite, a 1975 501).

SPECIFICATION	LOTUS ELITE 503
ENGINE	4 cylinders, dohc, 1973cc
HORSEPOWER	155bhp @ 6500rpm (later 160bhp)
TRANSMISSION	Manual 4-speed
CHASSIS	Backbone
SUSPENSION	Independent front and rear
BRAKES	Disc front, drum rear
TOP SPEED	200km/h (124mph)
ACCELERATION	0-96km/h (60mph): 7.8 seconds

construction was no longer questioned – the Elite passed crash tests without difficulty, and gained the Don Safety Trophy for Lotus in 1975.

However, the car's styling was never wholly accepted. This was the first four-seat Lotus, and thus inevitably larger than its predecessors, and in overall terms, wedge lines were combined with a hatchback layout. In the nose, the need for 5mph impact bumpers had to be taken into account, and retractable headlights again featured. The windscreen was steeply raked, and large, while the

flat rear panel seemed at odds with curves under the rear side windows. Boot space was reasonable.

The close-coupled interior was partly styled by Ital Design. While the chassis meant that there was a substantial centre divide, the greater overall width meant correspondingly more generous front seats, while the two small rear seats were habitable. Throughout the car, minor fittings were adapted from mass-production models – it was none the worse for that, but quality control fell short in some areas.

The basic version was the 501, while the 502 had a higher equipment level, appropriate to the customers Lotus sought. The 503 came for 1975, with air conditioning, power-assisted steering, electric windows and other enhancements. The 504 was the automatic transmission variant, fractionally slower than the normal cars, with a 191km/h (119mph) top speed.

Production had reached 2398 when these models gave way to the Elite 2.2 (Type 83) in Spring 1980. This had an oversquare 2174cc version of the engine, designated 912. It was still rated at 160bhp,

Above: The large flat rear window was a feature of the Elite. Late cars had a top-mounted wiper at the back.

but had greatly improved torque. A Getrag five-speed gearbox was adopted, with the Borg-Warner automatic still an option. In other respects, the 2.2 was equipped to 503 level.

Soon it was available to special order only, listed until the end of 1982. Average production was no more than one a week – actually one a month in Lotus' sales trough period in 1981-82 – and total 2.2 sales were 137.

Lotus Eclat

BEFORE its Autumn 1975 introduction, this model was regarded as the 'Elite coupé', and in almost all respects the Type 76 Eclat was an Elite variant. Generally, the base version was the cheapest car in the Lotus range in the second half of the 1970s, and in its 521 Sprint form, the Eclat was the fastest of the Elite/Eclat family. Incidentally, it shared the '76' number with a GP car.

The Eclat had fastback lines, sharing Elite body mouldings back to the doors. It was a 2+2 rather than a four-seater, and one with limited head room for rear-seat passengers. Mechanically, the basic model had a Ford four-speed gearbox, but others had Maxi-based five-speed 'boxes until a Getrag gearbox came with the Type 912 engine in the 2.2.

As with the Elite, options were not listed, but the car was offered in five forms: 520, base model, for which there was little demand; 521, uprated, with five-speed gearbox, wider alloy wheels and even a radio; 522, effectively the 521 with air conditioning and better accessories; 523, the 522 with power steering; 524, the automatic transmission version. Beyond that there were the Sprint 520 and 521, cosmetic special editions, save that the 521 Sprint had a lower axle ratio.

The 523 and 524 came in Spring 1976 and were listed for the next four years, when the 2.2 with the type number 84 was introduced, with a similar mechanical specification to the Elite 2.2. Like that car, it was to be offered in a Riviera special edition form with a lift-out roof panel, despite earlier resistance to any form of roof opening on the grounds that it could jeopardize structural integrity.

The cockpit was comfortable, save for that persistent Lotus shortcoming in the closeness of the pedals. The front seats reclined, and were supportive, although some leg room was sacrificed to gain rear-seat space.

Below and opposite above: Two views which emphasize similarities between the Elite and the fastback Eclat. This yellow car is an early Eclat.

The Eclat weighed just over 1100kg (2420lb), some 102kg (225lb) less than the Elite, and this was reflected in its better performance (perhaps aided by a marginal aerodynamic advantage). The Eclat 523 was 8km/h (5mph) faster than the Elite 503, while the 2.2 Sprint had a 209km/h (130mph) top speed.

The Eclat was discontinued in Summer 1982, when 1519 had been built; sales in the final two years were boosted by substantial price reductions. It was succeeded by the Excel.

SPECIFICATION	LOTUS ECLAT 523
ENGINE	4 cylinders, dohc, 1973cc
HORSEPOWER	160bhp @ 6200rpm
TRANSMISSION	Manual 5-speed
CHASSIS	Backbone
SUSPENSION	Independent front and rear
BRAKES	Disc front, drum rear
TOP SPEED	208km/h (129mph)
ACCELERATION	0-96km/h (60mph): 7.9 seconds

Below: A late Eclat 'Riviera' shows detail changes such as the nose-top outlets and fancy wheels, as well as the lift-out roof panel.

Lotus Esprit

THIS WAS destined to become the most significant Lotus since the company moved into the prestige GT market, and the model name was to last for more than two decades – the first Esprit (Type 79, confusingly sharing the number with an outstanding GP car) was launched in October 1979, and a V8 version came early in 1996. It was initiated as Project M70, but although a forerunner was exhibited at the Turin Motor Show in 1972, more than two years passed before it reached production.

It was always envisaged as a successor to the Europa, although it turned out to be much more than that. Following a chance meeting between Colin Chapman and Giorgetto Giugiaro of Ital Design at the Geneva Motor Show, a Europa that had already been modified in the M70 preliminaries was passed to the Italian designer, to follow up his proposals for a body for the new mid-engined GT car.

Giugiaro had made his name with his work for Bertone in the early 1960s, notably his Alfa Romeo coupés and the Iso Rivolta and Grifo. His first Ital Design work was for companies as diverse as Alfa Romeo and Mitsubishi. The silver Lotus exhibited at Turin surpassed any of these, and incidentally carried the name 'Esprit'.

Reactions were positive, and quickly led to a development programme, and a running prototype early in 1975. However, progress towards production was slow: financial resources were strained (Lotus Cars declared a trading loss in 1975), the broad design needed refinement, which took time, and a source of gearbox/final drive units had to be established – eventually, Citroën agreed to supply the

Below: Giugiaro's Ital Design concept car was a stunning 1972 show exhibit, and it inspired the Esprit.

transmission that had been developed with Maserati for the big front-wheel-drive SM and the Merak.

Under Giugiaro's striking body there was a backbone chassis, and this was used in the definitive Esprit but with no suggestion of 'forks' at each end. Instead there was a substantial box-section member to mount the front suspension and an angular sub-frame at the rear to carry engine, gearbox and

SPECIFICATION	LOTUS ESPRIT S1
ENGINE	4 cylinders, dohc, 1973cc
HORSEPOWER	160bhp @ 6200rpm
TRANSMISSION	Manual 5-speed
CHASSIS	Backbone
SUSPENSION	Independent front and rear
BRAKES	Disc
TOP SPEED	200km/h (124mph)
ACCELERATION	0-96km/h (60mph): 8.4 seconds

suspension. At the front this derived from the Opel Ascona, and there were no surprises at the rear. Rack-and-pinion steering was used, with no power assistance, and this Lotus had disc brakes all round, mounted inboard at the rear.

Top and above: The overall wedge lines of the S1 Esprit were remarkably close to Giugiaro's design, although there were naturally many detail improvements, for example in the rake of the windscreen. These two cars were photographed at Hethel.

49

Lotus' Type 907 engine, still rated at 160bhp, was canted at 45 degrees to the right, its exhaust side. The Citroën transmission unit was of course turned through 180 degrees, and fitted neatly under the rearmost cross member.

Broadly, Giugiaro laid out a balanced body on a wheelbase that was 100mm (4in) longer than the Europa's and 150mm (6in) wider in track. The overall lines followed Italian fashion of the period, with sharp edges, and, as it was a wide car, fortuitously with the conspicuous waist line that came with Lotus' method of body construction.

At the nose, an effective chin spoiler was prominent below the black bumper moulding with its inset parking lights and turn indicators (this took the place of the chrome bumper on Giugiaro's original car). The headlights were in two pairs, on electrically-operated retractable panels. The louvres atop the nose of the 1972 car were abandoned, and radiator air was exhausted under the car. A nose compartment housed a spare front wheel and tools, allowing space for a little soft luggage. Wheels were 6J at the front, 7J at the rear.

The windscreen was less steeply raked in the production version, giving good visibility to the front, save that the nose was out of sight and the pillars seemed thick. The habitual Lotus GT shortcoming in terms of three-quarter rear vision was perpetuated. A large hatch gave access to the rear compartment, where a plastic engine cover bulged into the luggage space (in volume terms, this was roughly three-quarters the size of the Eclat boot).

The cockpit was designed for two people, and for their immediate belongings there was just a glove box and a small space behind the gear lever. The semi-reclining seats with built-in headrests were

Below: Most of the changes in the Esprit S2 were under the skin, and minor. Outwardly, the spoiler under the nose was integrated into the bodywork and 'Esprit S2' appeared on the rear quarters.

50

comfortable, with fore-and-aft adjustment as the large steering wheel and column were fixed on this model. The fascia pod ahead of the wheel turned out to be more practical than it appeared to be at first sight in 1972: instruments were seen through the wheel, while the ends of the pod were angled towards the driver, with minor controls logically arranged (only the choke and window lift switches were on the centre line, behind the gear lever).

Contributions to strength and safety included

Above: The S3 was also identified at the rear (although the 'S' was omitted). The sills, nose spoiler and the neat intakes behind the rear windows are in the body colour. This car has BBS wheels.

a box-section cross member mounted to the backbone and linking the A posts carrying the doors, aluminium box sections in the doors, serving other purposes as in the Elite/Elan, and a firewall-cum-bulkhead between cockpit and engine compartment.

SPECIFICATION	LOTUS ESPRIT S3
ENGINE	4 cylinders, dohc, 2174cc
HORSEPOWER	160bhp @ 6500rpm
TRANSMISSION	Manual 5-speed
CHASSIS	Backbone
SUSPENSION	Independent front and rear
BRAKES	Disc
TOP SPEED	217km/h (135mph)
ACCELERATION	0-96km/h (60mph): 8 seconds

Limited production got under way in 1976, increasing as a Federal version came in 1977 (like the US market Elite, this had a 140bhp engine).

These cars did not wholly live up to their promise. Handling, traction and braking were rated very highly, but the Esprit was criticized in several respects: from poor finish to noise, from poor ventilation to visibility. Independent tests never confirmed the claimed 220km/h (137mph) top speed, S1 cars achieving 201km/h (125mph), or 193km/h (120mph) in Federal form.

One outcome was the development of the S2, little more than two years after the first Esprits had been delivered (718 were built). Changes were not extensive. Outwardly, the attractive Wolfrace cast aluminium wheels gave way to Speedline wheels, the nose spoiler was integrated into the bodywork and more effectively directed air to the radiator, adjustable door mirrors were an overdue standard fitting, there were intakes behind the side windows, and there were new rear lights. Road tested by *Autocar*, an Esprit S2 was estimated to be capable of 217km/h (135mph). In two years, the price of an Esprit had increased by almost 50 per cent . . .

S2 production reached 1148, with the Esprit 2.2 coming in Spring 1980, and the S3 with minor changes a year later, to run on until 1987. The 2.2 had the enlarged 912 engine introduced in contemporary front-engined models, offering no more peak power but greatly improved torque.

Meanwhile, an Esprit with considerably more power, the Turbo, had been announced early in 1980, although it was not available until late Summer. As an aside, an independent turbo conversion had been marketed in 1978 by Bell and Colvill. Carried out by Mathwall, this used a Garrett turbocharger, which in turn called for modifications at the rear. Bell and Colvill claimed a 241km/h (150mph) capability, and there were benefits in acceleration and flexibility, gained at a disproportionate financial cost.

Two Esprits (and an Excel) served as test beds in Lotus' active suspension research; the conversion of one of the Esprits was comprehensive in the SID (Structures, Isolation and Dynamics) programme. It was distinguished by its extended tail and the deletion of side windows – and the complete absence of roll as it changed direction.

Left: Essex Petroleum sponsorship of the Lotus racing teams led to the garish colour scheme seen on this 1980 Esprit Turbo, a special edition car with detail aerodynamic refinements. It also had slats over the engine.

SPECIFICATION	LOTUS ESPRIT TURBO (1980)
ENGINE	4 cylinders, dohc, Garrett turbo, 2174cc
HORSEPOWER	210bhp @ 6000rpm
TRANSMISSION	Manual 5-speed
CHASSIS	Backbone
SUSPENSION	Independent front and rear
BRAKES	Disc
TOP SPEED	238km/h (148mph)
ACCELERATION	0-96km/h (60mph): 6.1 seconds

Below and right: Most of the outward features, such as the deeper nose aerofoil and ducts low down ahead of the rear wheels, were carried over to later Esprits, such as this 1987 Turbo HC.

Esprit Turbo

The mainstream 'Essex Commemorative Turbo Esprit' appeared in the petroleum company's garish colours, announced with the 1980 racing cars it sponsored. In the Turbo Esprit (Project M72, Type 82) there was no question of simply bolting on a turbocharger. The car was extensively re-engineered.

The engine was the long-stroke 2.2, converted to dry-sump lubrication (in 1983 the Turbo reverted to wet-sump lubrication). The Garrett turbo was mounted behind the block and above the clutch, with a low waste gate. Carburettors were still used, and the inlet boost was 8psi. The compression ratio was reduced from 9.2:1 to 7.5:1. Claimed peak power was 210bhp, while torque was 200lb ft at 4500rpm, compared with the normal 2.2's 160lb ft at 5000rpm.

Little more space was needed, but the frame at the rear of the chassis was substantially modified (in part, it was admitted, anticipating a V8). New drive shafts did not have a suspension role as a top link was introduced, and one advantage of this was that vibrations were no longer fed through the transmission to the rest of the car. There were fewer Opel components in the front suspension.

In the body there were aerodynamic refinements, with a larger nose spoiler, side skirts with NACA duct intakes for engine air, and a rear spoiler. The drag figure was a little poorer, at 0.36. There was a new bumper at the back, while the rear window gave way to louvres.

Inside, generous use of soft leather seemed to transform the cockpit, but there was little real change beyond the addition of a turbo boost gauge, and the oddity of a hi-fi system mounted to the centre of the roof – customer reaction meant this was soon dropped, and in any case a detachable glass sun roof was to become optional.

The claimed top speed was 244km/h (152mph), and the first *Autocar* test came close to this, recording 238km/h (148mph). The Turbo was cleaned up for its US introduction in 1983, when little power was sacrificed in de-toxing the engine and performance was hardly affected.

Below: The lines of the Peter Stevens-styled Esprit that came in 1987 were still evident in the 1990s (this is a 1993 S4).

SPECIFICATION	LOTUS ESPRIT S4
ENGINE	4 cylinders, dohc, Garrett turbo, 2174cc
HORSEPOWER	264bhp @ 6500rpm
TRANSMISSION	Manual 5-speed
CHASSIS	Backbone
SUSPENSION	Independent front and rear
BRAKES	Disc
TOP SPEED	260km/h (161mph)
ACCELERATION	0-96km/h (60mph): 4.9 seconds

Left: The 'new-style' Esprit was more rounded, and this was particularly noticeable in the carefully-integrated nose features.
Below: The Esprit Sport 300, here at the 1992 British Motor Show, could be used on public roads and also be equipped for competition, for example with a roll cage.

Suspension and brakes were modified for 1985, Toyota providing ventilated front discs, but the next significant change came with the 1987 Esprit Turbo HC (high compression). Boost as well as compression ratio was increased, and there was a modest power uprating.

New Lines

The 18-month X180 programme brought substantial changes late in 1987, with the normally-aspirated Esprit and Esprit Turbo sharing a new body. In this house design by Peter Stevens the sharp lines gave way to a smoother and rounded

Left: The Esprit S4 – here in S4S form – and the X180R circuit car broadly shared the same chassis and body. The X180Rs were very successful in US racing, and Doc Bundy drove this car to win an IMSA championship in 1992.
Below: The Esprit GT3 was a basic 2-litre model introduced to complement the Esprit V8 in 1996. It gained high praise for its all-round driving qualities.

appearance, while the side elevation profile remained. The car looked longer as well as sleeker, yet dimensional changes were minimal. The Cd figure that had crept up with wider tyres was back to 0.36.

The body was still made in two main portions, but formed by the VARI process (Vacuum Assisted Resin Injection), which offered time and labour savings, as well as greater uniformity – useful, as Lotus made determined efforts further to improve build quality. Kevlar reinforcement was incorporated, especially in the flanks. The body was bolted to the chassis, and the suspension was unchanged.

The normally-aspirated engine was rated at 172bhp, the turbo unit at 215bhp, and that figure was quoted for US market cars with Bosch K-Jetronic fuel injection in place of carburettors – the difference was in DIN and SAE horses. A Renault GTA transaxle replaced the Citroën unit. Rear brakes were relocated inboard. Weight was increased by some 240kg (530lb), but the new Esprit was no slower – 222km/h (138mph) was claimed for the normally-aspirated car, while road testers achieved 245km/h (152mph) in the Turbo.

The cockpit was essentially familiar, restyled by Simon Cox and with new instruments, but with the old failings.

Detail changes came in 1988, when there was a 40th anniversary Esprit Turbo in white; then in Spring 1989 the Turbo SE was announced. With a high-boost, pressure-charged engine rated at 264bhp, this had a 264km/h (164mph) top speed. There were some chassis changes, revised sills and spoilers, and the Delco ABS braking system that Lotus had worked on for GM became available for the Esprit. In this form, it became S4 in 1993, and at last power steering was standardized.

Meanwhile, Lotus had returned to sports car racing, supporting a Turbo SE team in the USA, and gaining four victories in a national Showroom Stock series.

The Esprit Sport 300 followed, based on the racing X180R, announced late in 1992 and in production in May 1993, just before two were run at Le Mans, Lotus' first works-associated entry in the 24-hour race since Chapman turned away from it in 1962, when his 23s were rejected on a flimsy pretext. Neither car finished in 1993.

The Sport 300 weighed 35kg (77lb) less than the normal S4, and had a reworked 2.2 litre engine, with modified head and inlet valves and a Garrett T3/T4 turbocharger, rated at 306bhp in 1995. There were aerodynamic and suspension modifications, and provision for a competitions roll cage.

It was successful in national race series in several countries in 1994-95. In 1995 Lotus contested an international GT series, and an in-house programme got under way, aimed at the 1996 season with a development of the Lotus 114 with a competitions version of the V8.

The Sport 300 led to the S4S in October 1994, to fall between the S4 and the Sport 300 in a three-model Esprit range (the 'Turbo' name was dropped when the normally-aspirated model was discontinued after 385 SEs had been built). It used the extended wheel arches and rear wing from the Sport 300, while cockpit trim changes and a new instrument pack were shared with the S4. With a Garrett T3/60 turbo, the S4S engine was rated at 186bhp, giving a claimed top speed of 260km/h (161mph). Esprit sales increased in 1995. Then the 2.2 litre engine was phased out, in anticipation of the V8 and the 2-litre development for the GT3, as well as emissions regulations.

Below: The Esprit V8 retained the existing body, with the new power unit slipping neatly into the existing engine space. The five-spoke wheels are distinctive.

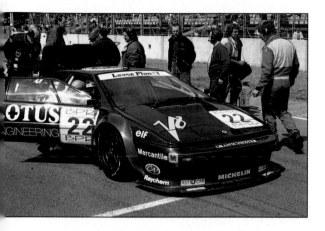

Above: One of the Lotus Racing Team Esprit GT1s on the grid for the 1996 British Empire Trophy race at Silverstone.

Esprit V8

A 4-litre V8 for the Etna of 1984-85 was never developed as a production unit (when the Etna project car appeared, it had been expected to become a 290km/h [180mph] supercar, in production by 1988). The Lotus V8 that at last broke cover in March 1996 is a 90 degree 3.5 litre unit, with two Garrett T25 turbochargers, stiff and compact, and weighing 210kg (462lb), only 15 per cent more than the 2.2 litre four-cylinder unit. Importantly, it has comprehensive engine management and diagnostics systems, and meets the stringent US emissions rules that came in 1996. Designated 618, it is also intended for sale to other manufacturers. In its first road-car application, it is modestly rated at 349bhp, but the racing version with a single intercooled turbocharger produced some 520bhp for its first events.

The GT1 circuit car actually appeared first,

looking purposeful with prominent aerofoils at nose and tail, and large wheel arch extensions. There is a new chassis, a six-speed sequential gearbox and carbon brakes, while the car is down to the 900kg (1984lbs) weight limit. It showed promise in its Global Endurance GT series debut, but suffered teething problems before its first top-three placing, second at Silverstone in May.

The road Esprit V8 on Lotus' 1996 Geneva Motor Show stand carried V8 badges, had a new front valance, bigger engine air intakes and outlets, six-spoke alloy wheels and twin exhausts, but no other external clues to changes under the skin, such as a stiffer chassis and a new Kelsey-Hayes ABS braking system. US-specification cars have a mid-mounted rear wing, rather than the aerofoil curving gracefully down to end mountings on the bodywork. There are few cockpit changes, beyond a 300km/h (186mph) speedo and improved air conditioning equipment.

The top speed is a certified 282km/h (175mph), which lifts the Esprit into the top twenty among supercars, while the claimed 0-100km/h (0-62mph) acceleration time is 4.5 seconds.

As the V8 was announced, a new entry-level Esprit GT3 was shown in prototype form, well ahead of its proposed European introduction date in Autumn 1996. The equipment standard is basic, and it recalls earlier Esprits in its clean lines, particularly at the rear where there is a modest lip instead of a 'wing'. The engine is a 2-litre development of the four-cylinder unit. Claimed top speed is 262km/h (163mph) – supercar performance on a par with the Aston Martin DB7 or Ferrari 348GTS.

With this Esprit pair, Lotus could look forward to the 25th year since the name first appeared on Giugiaro's show-stopping project car . . .

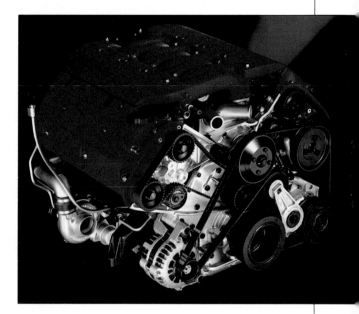

Above: The compact and light Lotus 618 V8 engine.

SPECIFICATION	LOTUS ESPRIT V8
ENGINE	V8, dohc, two Garrett turbochargers, 3506cc
HORSEPOWER	349bhp @ 6500rpm
TRANSMISSION	Manual 5-speed
CHASSIS	Backbone
SUSPENSION	Independent front and rear
BRAKES	Disc
TOP SPEED	Claimed 282km/h (175mph)
ACCELERATION	0-96km/h (60mph): 4.5 seconds

Overall impressions of the Esprit V8 (below and opposite) are of a purposeful GT car. Compared with earlier Esprits there is a new nose valance with a larger air intake. This European-spec car has the rear wing from the Esprit S4; cars for the USA have a mid-mounted wing. There are twin tail pipes, and a discreet V8 badge alongside the number plate (far right). Cockpit fittings largely derive from the S4, although there is an 180mph (290km/h) speedo and 'V8' on the rev counter.

60

Lotus Excel

T HE EXCEL was first known as Eclat 3, then as the Eclat Excel, which meant that the Type Approval process was avoided. There were rewarding style changes as well as some mechanical uprating through the use of Toyota components. It was built in modest numbers, 1982-92, with the definitive body coming late in 1984, when the Eclat name was discarded.

Project M55, which was to become Type 89, Excel, was economic in development and build terms. Customer preference for more aggressive lines gave designer Peter Stevens a cue, and was to

be achieved without change to the lower half of the body, the doors and some lesser parts. Thus one of the two major moulds was retained.

Mechanically, the suspension was modified, and Toyota ventilated disc brakes were introduced. Toyota also provided the gearbox, final drive and drive shafts, all from the Supra (the coupé Supra had some Lotus input).

Outwardly, the nose was softer than the Eclat's, with bumper, spoiler, intakes and secondary lights neatly integrated. The wheel arches were altered and the rear side windows were changed and

more in sympathy with the boot lines. The boot had a larger aperture, and there were minor modifications at the rear, for example revised spoilers in 1985 and 1989, the first to cure a slight aerodynamic imbalance. The revisions were proved in wind tunnels, and the definitive Excel had a better Cd figure than the Eclat; it was down to 0.32 for 1986, when a new rear spoiler was introduced.

The cockpit was smarter, and overhauled late in 1985, when there was a new fascia with VDO instruments. Rear-seat passengers had a little more head room, but access was still difficult.

Below: The front-engined Lotus GT line was extended with the Excel. Heavy bumpers marred US-market cars.
Right: Badges on the tail explicitly defined its origins.

The engine was uprated for the SE in 1986, with higher compression ratio, 'tri-jet' carburettors, improved breathing and tweaks including a reprofiled camshaft, leading to an output of 180bhp. In this form the Excel was slightly quicker, even if its top speed fell below Lotus' own 217km/h (135mph) claim.

At the same time, the Excel SA (Sport Automatic) was introduced with a ZF four-speed automatic transmission. *Autocar* testers compared its performance with the manual transmission SE, inevitably finding that it was inferior, for example in acceleration (respective 0-100mph times were 24.9 seconds and 19.9 seconds). Top speed was 200km/h (124mph).

The fuel-injection engine was never fitted to a production Excel, and this meant that it was not listed in some markets.

There were minor changes through to the end of the 1980s, even though sales tailed off from 1988. This dual-purpose GT or sports car was listed until 1992, when the last 15 were built to bring the total production to 1327. Its passing meant the end of a line of front-engined Lotus cars – Elite, Eclat and Excel.

SPECIFICATION	LOTUS EXCEL SE
ENGINE	4 cylinders, dohc, 2174cc
HORSEPOWER	180bhp @ 6500rpm
TRANSMISSION	Manual 5-speed
CHASSIS	Backbone
SUSPENSION	Independent front and rear
BRAKES	Disc
TOP SPEED	211km/h (131mph)
ACCELERATION	0-96km/h (60mph): 6.8 seconds

Below: Leather was prominent in many Lotus GT cockpits. This is an Excel SA, with ZF automatic transmission.

Lotus Elan

LOTUS returned to the small sports-car market with this car in Autumn 1989. But it came after false starts – the convoluted background can only be traced in outline here – and at best it was modestly successful. In the 1970s Colin Chapman just did not want a successor to the original Elan, and stipulated that this project should be undertaken only with the collaboration of a major manufacturer. So it did not start to take shape before the 1981 agreement with Toyota.

M90 was envisaged as front-engined, rear-drive car using Toyota dohc 16-valve engines and running gear, initially a two-seater, but with 2+2 and three-door derivatives to follow. Toyota was enthusiastic; once the styling mock-up and single uninspired prototype were seen, Lotus executive reactions were mixed.

Work was in any case halted for almost a year after Colin Chapman's death, then picked up with a radically different concept, code-named X100. This was a small front-wheel-drive car, drawing on ride and handling work Lotus had undertaken with that layout for other manufacturers. It was still to use Toyota components, with a body on the lines of the Etna project car of 1984. By the end of 1985 the general lines and rather different styling had been agreed, design and development work started, only to be cancelled in March 1986.

That was a month after GM took control; later in the year a project coded M100 was approved at Hethel, and GM rubber-stamped the go-ahead. In place of Toyota, there was to be an association with Isuzu, particularly in sourcing the power train. Front-wheel drive was retained. The body was the subject of the first-ever Lotus design competition, and the two-seat convertible designed in-house was chosen.

MD Michael Kimberley regarded this car as a 'flagship for Lotus Engineering', but then he had always wanted an Elan successor. He rated the new car important to the target of increasing production from 1300 units a year to 4500 by the mid-1990s. He also insisted that it was not over-complicated, yet it had involved heavy investment, in new technology as well as design and development, and it was to prove difficult and costly to make – factors that were to be reflected in high prices . . .

There was a backbone chassis, from the bulkhead to the rear suspension pick-up points, but in this Elan it was combined with a body platform, a VARI-moulded sub-structure with steel sills and outriggers riveted and bonded to it. This was rigid in itself, and there were additional steel cross members, which also provided side impact protection. A front sub-frame assembly incorporating suspension and engine mountings was bolted to the front of the backbone. The body shell of reinforced VARI panels was mounted to the sub-structure, and outer panels were not stressed.

The independent rear suspension was straightforward, but the front suspension called for intensive development. An 'interactive wishbone'

Above: The Isuzu-Lotus twin-cam fuel-injected turbo engine was a tight fit under the Elan bonnet.

system was devised; basically this was a double wishbone arrangement, with the assembly on each side mounted to a cast aluminium alloy 'raft'. It was claimed that this made for accurate wheel control, and accurate control of suspension geometry under all conditions, for minimal steering effort and reduced torque steer. There were unusually long coil spring/damper units, and a tubular anti-roll bar.

The cam covers of the engine were labelled 'Isuzu-Lotus', but there was little Lotus input. The iron-block unit had Rochester fuel injection and while a few Elans were sold with normally-aspirated 130bhp engines, most had the 165bhp version with an IHI turbocharger. Claimed top speeds were 195km/h (121mph) and 220km/h (137mph) respectively.

Below: With its short nose, steeply raked windscreen and relatively wide track, the Elan seemed a stubby little car after a series of sleek Lotus GT models, and its Cd figures were not outstanding. It was also clever and complex, and that meant higher prices. The cockpit (right) was not spacious, but ergonomically it was efficient. The fat steering wheel hides the main instruments, rev counter on the left and central speedometer.

SPECIFICATION	LOTUS ELAN SE
ENGINE	4 cylinders, dohc, IHI turbocharger, 1588cc
HORSEPOWER	165bhp @ 6600rpm
TRANSMISSION	Manual 5-speed
CHASSIS	Backbone, with front longeron/underframe
SUSPENSION	Independent front and rear
BRAKES	Disc
TOP SPEED	220km/h (137mph)
ACCELERATION	0-96km/h (60mph): 6.6 seconds

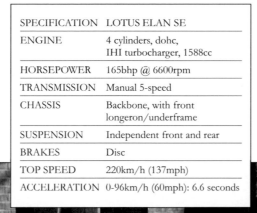

65

Most Lotus road cars have looked sleek. The Elan was different – the transverse engine, the 'cab-forward' layout, short low nose and high rear body line, and Peter Stevens' rounded treatment, contributed its unusual overall appearance (incidentally, Elans for the US market were 63.5mm [2.5in] longer than European-specification cars, because of the impact-resistant bumpers, and in some ways this enhanced the nose lines). Air was ducted under the front bumper to radiator, intercooler and brakes.

The appearance of this Elan may have been controversial, but apart from restricted lateral room, the cockpit was generally well received – there was even reasonable stowage space, in a glove box, door pockets and a centre console storage area. The fascia panel had a non-reflecting single-piece cover over the main analogue instruments. The soft top was stowed under a flush cover; erected, it did not look elegant, nor did it always seal properly. Hood up, the drag coefficient was 0.34. A neat hard top was listed after a year.

Road test reactions were enthusiastic, and most journalists who were prejudiced against front-wheel-drive sports cars were won over, especially by the Elan's extraordinary capability in point to point journeys over secondary roads. Generally, performance claims for the turbocharged version were confirmed.

Below: The Elan re-emerged in 1994 in this S2 guise. This car is driven by John Miles, one-time GP driver who has played a significant role in developing Lotus models.

But – and it is a very big 'but' – the SE was priced at almost £20,000, or $40,000 in the important US market, and that was just not competitive. Production really got under way in 1990, but sales never matched forecasts.

A decision to end Elan production was widely expected little more than two years after the car's announcement, and it came in June 1992, seemingly as no Lotus or GM executives were prepared to fight its corner. Production reached 3857, and presumably the Elan contributed substantially to Lotus' trading losses.

However, the end of the story had yet to be written. In August 1993 Bugatti bought Group Lotus from GM, and later that year it was announced that 'a special limited-edition run of the Lotus Elan will be built next year'. Bugatti people found among the Hethel assets the Elan tooling, 800 crated Isuzu power trains, and a dark area of the plant that could be brought back to life.

So the Elan S2 appeared in the 1994 Geneva Motor Show, with a commitment to build 450 in right-hand-drive form, and 350 as left-hand-drive cars. Over a hundred improvements were claimed. Outwardly, the larger wheels (16in alloys in place of 15in) distinguished it, there were associated suspension and steering detail changes, the hood was revised and more efficient. The kerb weight was increased from 997kg (2198lb) to 1060kg (2337lb), and unfortunately this went hand in hand with a 10bhp loss of power, as a catalytic converter was a standard fitment. Acceleration suffered – the S2 needed an extra four seconds to reach 100mph, or 161km/h – while the top speed was down to 211km/h (131mph).

Above: The cockpit of the first Elan S2. Right: Kia showed KMS II in Europe in 1996 as a concept car, although a similar Elan derivative was in production for its home market.

More than half the run was sold within months of the announcement, and in August 1995 the last Elan was completed, only 18 days before the Elise was unveiled.

Some further development was put into the car, on behalf of Kia. The Korean company also took over some tooling, to produce its own sports car. This had many resemblances, but as many differences, as for example the chassis had to be adapted for a Kia engine and transmission.

Lotus Carlton/Omega

Above: Lotus-developed and badged turbocharged engine gave this four-door saloon performance in the supercar class.

THIS astonishing car was as important to Lotus as the 1990s opened as the Lotus-Cortina had been in the 1960s, and it gave the General Motors European marques an ultra-high performance saloon – it was badged Vauxhall (Carlton) or Opel (Omega), while its Lotus type number was M104. Unlike the Lotus-Cortina, or the rallying Talbot Sunbeam Lotus of 1978, there were no competitions objectives; this was a five-seater that could out-perform most so-called supercars.

The start point was the top-of-the-range Opel Omega, the 3000 24V, regardless of subsequent Vauxhall badging on right-hand-drive cars. Complete German vehicles were sent to Hethel for conversion – total rebuilds gives a truer impression. Opel's own transformation of its straight six was fundamental. In the 3000 24V, this was a 3-litre 204bhp unit; for use in the Lotus, the bore (marginally) and stroke were increased to raise capacity to 3.6 litres, there was a new twin-cam cylinder head, and twin Garrett T25 intercooled turbochargers were added, to give an output of 377bhp.

To cope with the tremendous torque (419lb at 4200rpm), the six-speed ZF gearbox from the Chevrolet Corvette ZR-1 was adopted, although the very high ratio sixth gear was really superfluous. There was a limited-slip differential.

The suspension had to be uprated, with self-levelling at the rear, while the ventilated disc brakes echoed sports-racing car practices. Body changes included a front spoiler and rear wing, modest skirts below the sills, and wheel arch extensions to accommodate the fat alloy wheels and low profile tyres. The drag factor was an excellent 0.31.

The interior was overhauled, most noticeably with new seats and instruments.

It was announced at the 1989 Geneva Motor Show, but more than a year passed before cars were delivered. It was listed until 1992, but sales were sluggish and the original build target of 1100 units was not reached (some 440 were completed as Vauxhalls, while the Opel total was apparently a little higher). A Lotus Omega was the basis of Pininfarina's 1991 Chronos concept car.

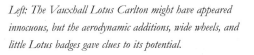

Left: The Vauxhall Lotus Carlton might have appeared innocuous, but the aerodynamic additions, wide wheels, and little Lotus badges gave clues to its potential.

68

In its time, this was the fastest five-seater saloon ever built, with a maximum speed to match a Lamborghini Countach – and usable qualities that car never had – with excellent handling characteristics and reassuring safety advantages.

Performance? GM admitted to 283km/h (176mph) recorded at an Italian test track, and to 0-100km/h (62mph) acceleration in 5.4 seconds, or 0-

SPECIFICATION	LOTUS CARLTON/OMEGA
ENGINE	6 cylinders, dohc, two Garrett turbochargers, 3638cc
HORSEPOWER	377bhp @ 5200rpm
TRANSMISSION	Manual 6-speed
CHASSIS	Unitary
SUSPENSION	Independent front and rear
BRAKES	Disc
TOP SPEED	283km/h (176mph)
ACCELERATION	0-96km/h (60mph): 5.1 seconds

161km/h (100mph) in 10.9 seconds. On the road, it was timed at over 280km/h (174mph). It was a demonstration of Lotus Engineering capabilities, and a remarkable flagship for General Motors in Europe.

Below: Opel Lotus Omega was the left-hand-drive variant (this one seemingly featuring both a British tax disc and a German plate!).

Lotus Elise

THE ELISE marks a return to basic Lotus philosophies: it is innovative and light, it has a very stiff chassis to combine with the suspension to give optimum handling and ride, it echoes racing practices in some respects and it is straightforward in production terms.

The design team led by Julian Thomson started work in January 1994, encouraged by Romano Artioli despite the problems hanging over his Italian Bugatti company – the Lotus 111 was to be named after his grand-daughter, Elise. The first prototype was completed at the end of 1994 and the European Whole Vehicle Type Approval was granted in September 1995, shortly before the car's launch at the Frankfurt Motor Show. Then, in a Lotus tradition of long lead times between announcement and sales, the first production cars were not scheduled to be delivered until 'late Spring 1996', which later drifted to Summer 1996. But the initial annual rate of 700 units suggested prudent forecasts after the over-optimism of the Elan launch, and there was the reassurance after the main Autumn 1995 shows that the first 18 months' production was spoken for, although early in 1996 that had been trimmed back to a year's production.

As the Elise was launched, the open two-seater had found renewed favour with several manufacturers, after years when this market niche

Above: The chassis of the Elise is highly original; constructed from epoxy-bonded aluminium extrusions, it is both light and strong. Below left: Designer Julian Thompson with an Elise on a motor show turntable late in 1995.

had been largely neglected. Its looks might not have been universally praised, but in specification the Elise was well ahead of more conventional models in the class, and in all-round performance could have an important edge.

The Elise is the first production road car to have a chassis of epoxy-bonded aluminium extrusions (the otherwise similar Renault Spider Sport had a welded chassis from the same Danish source, Hydro Aluminium Automotive Suppliers). Lotus' construction ensures extremely close tolerances, meets all safety requirements (in particular, the main side beams are very substantial and a roll-over hoop is built in), makes for torsional rigidity and promises durability. It weighs a mere 65kg (143lb). Lotus literature refers to it as a space

SPECIFICATION	LOTUS ELISE
ENGINE	4 cylinders, dohc, 1796cc
HORSEPOWER	Approx 125bhp @ 5500rpm
TRANSMISSION	Manual 5-speed
CHASSIS	Space frame
SUSPENSION	Independent front and rear
BRAKES	Disc
TOP SPEED	Estimated 201km/h (126mph)
ACCELERATION	0-96km/h (60mph): 7.6 seconds

frame and although at first sight it looks far removed from the traditional assembly of round tubes, its main members are hollow and they are in three dimensions, while the floor is not a structural member – it is perhaps halfway between a ladder frame and a space frame ('a highly-derived space frame' is one Lotus explanation).

The extrusion process is used to produce other parts, such as pedals and suspension uprights. The double wishbone suspension is familiar, but the

Above: Few small sports cars look elegant with the soft top erected – the hard top, announced late in 1996, was a more attractive means of weather-proofing an Elise – but in this case the soft top does mate well to the wind-up windows, and it stows behind the seats when it is not in use so that it does not take up luggage space.

Lanxide aluminium metal matrix composites brake discs are novel, and are claimed to offer good heat dissipation, as well as low weight.

Below and opposite: At rest the Elise promises outstanding sports car performance. . . Front and rear, its lines are rounded, although in some respects it is not altogether elegant. The VARI mouldings are of the highest quality, and shut lines are precise. Incidentally, the same orange indicator lights are used at both ends, and the driving lights inset in the nose of this car are optional. The seats (right) hardly look adequate, but they are. Some cockpit width is sacrificed to the wide sills. The main instruments (far right) seen through the Lotus/Nardi wheel are an electronic rev counter with multi-function LCD read-out and a speedometer with assorted warning lights.

The mid-mounted engine is the Rover 1.8i K-series unit, rated some 5bhp higher than its 120bhp MGF form, but considerably below the 200bhp which the chassis, running gear and plumbing can apparently cope with. Drive to the rear wheels is through a five-speed transaxle.

The composites body is an in-house design, with its aerodynamic efficiency proved in wind-tunnel work (but its detailing, if not overall lines, have never been to every taste, with some critics detecting retro elements). Splitters below the main lights and a rear lip combat lift, while an optional ducted undertray generates downforce. Eye-catching

features are the large outlets ahead of the windscreen and the side intakes coupled with sculpted channels in the doors. Wind-up windows are a concession to comfort, and there is a simple soft top.

The cockpit can be fitted out in left- or right-hand-drive form with minimal changes; in either form, the driver's seat is fully adjustable and slightly nearer the centre line than the fixed passenger seat. Ahead of the Lotus-Nardi steering wheel the electronic speedo and tacho are prominent. Entry over the large side members can be challenging. The luggage space behind the engine is hardly generous (there is a common front-hinged cover).

With an unladen weight of only 675kg (1488lb), the Elise is well ahead of its class rivals in power/weight ratio terms. The front-rear weight distribution is 39/61.

In some visual respects, this Lotus may not be elegant, but that quality was never claimed for the Seven, and – although this was presumably not part of the design group's brief – the Elise can be seen as a 1990s car in the mould of the Seven. Like that immortal, it is a purposeful all-round sports car, with a basic specification that suggests it is well-suited to its dual roles on road and track. And it neatly complements the Esprits in the Lotus range.

Lotus Cars MD, Rod Mansfield, suggested at its launch that 'this car typifies what Lotus has done best for almost forty years', while Romano Artioli suggested that this new Lotus 'reflected the genius of Colin Chapman'. Although he had been taking his company in other directions for a quarter of a century, one suspects that Colin Chapman might well have approved of the Elise . . .

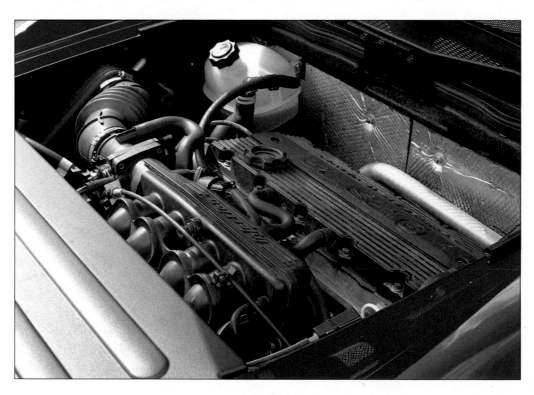

Left: The neat Elise engine installation, in a car on the production line. Opposite top left: The Elise Sprint, introduced late in 1996, is a stripped version, some 20kg (44lb) lighter than the normal car and with a deflector instead of a windscreen. Opposite top right: Cockpit of the Lotus Elise Sprint at the British Motor Show, in 1996. Opposite below: For serious international racing, Lotus' 1997 GT1 uses the Elise chassis, strengthened with a roll cage, and with a tubular rear section. The engine is the 3.5 litre twin-turbo V8, giving some 550bhp in race trim, and driving through a six-speed gearbox. GT racing regulations mean that a road version is also offered – at a dauntingly high price.

A Racing Postscript

RACING was such a powerful motivating force through most of the Lotus story that it cannot be ignored. Most Lotus types – more than 80 – have been intended for competitions use, reflecting Colin Chapman's over-riding interest. Some were failures, but some were landmark designs. And that makes Team Lotus' decline in the 1980s, to eventual obliteration in January 1995, particularly sad.

For two decades, Lotus was the dominant force in Grand Prix racing: between 1960 and 1979 it won 71 World Championship races, far more than any other constructor in this period. Its total was to be 79 victories; it won the Constructors' title seven times; it won the Indianapolis 500; its cars were mightily successful in secondary categories.

Racing cars were built for sale through to 1971, when Lotus Racing Limited was closed. Sales were sluggish by then, and Chapman wanted to concentrate on Team Lotus' Formula 1 activities. The Lotus Racing plant was used by the Team for a while, until it was moved to Ketteringham Hall in 1972. It was to be increasingly distanced from Group Lotus in the 1980s, so that by 1986 the association was in name only.

Below: Colin Chapman proudly showing off a marvellous collection of his Players-sponsored Grand Prix cars (and some transporters!) at Brands Hatch in 1981.

The first Lotus to win a World Championship race was an 18 in 1960, the last was a 99T in 1987. In the years between, four Lotus types were to stand out, technically and in victories – they were driven to win 59 championship races.

Lotus 25 and 33

Colin Chapman's first mid-engined racing car, the 18, was straightforward, the 21 was a refined derivative, the 24 an advanced space-frame car. But this method of construction was very quickly overtaken as the 25 brought the monocoque hull into modern GP racing in 1962.

Below: Jim Clark leaning to Copse Corner at Silverstone in a spindly Lotus 25 GP car in 1963. The car wears the traditional Team Lotus colours.

Right: A Lotus 49 in Gold Leaf Team Lotus colours in B form during the brief period when high aerofoil devices were permitted. Driver is Graham Hill, in the 1968 British GP.

The 25 was not the first circuit car with at least partial monocoque construction, but it was the first significant single-seater with it. In effect, Chapman envisaged his backbone chassis spread to accommodate a cockpit. In the 1.5-litre 25, this took the form of side pontoons (which contained the fuel tanks) linked by the floor, bulkheads and fascia panel frame. It was more rigid than a space frame, which meant that more supple suspension could be used and that made for superior cornering, while it was also lighter and much more crash-resistant. In this car, it was open at the top (hence the type became known as a 'bathtub' monocoque), enclosed

by notably sleek plastics bodywork. The 33 was a development of the 25, appearing in 1964.

The 25 and 33 are forever associated with Jim Clark – the brilliant Scot won 20 Grands Prix in them, as well as the Drivers' Championship in 1963 and 1965.

Lotus 49

For the 49, Chapman persuaded Ford to back the development of the Cosworth DFV 3-litre V8, and this was the first racing car of the modern era to use the engine as a load-bearing chassis member – it was bolted to the bulkhead behind the cockpit, while the rear suspension was mounted to its block and cylinder head. During its four-year, front-line life, the 49 was also central to the development of strut-mounted aerofoils ('wings') and their abrupt demise. It was the first GP car to appear in a sponsor's colours (another Chapman enterprise) and Rob Walker's 49, driven by Jo Siffert, was the last private-entrant car to win a Grand Prix, the 1968 British race.

Jim Clark gave the 49 a debut race victory in 1967, Jochen Rindt scored its 12th championship race victory in 1970. In between, Graham Hill won his second world title with 49s in 1968, and his fifth Monaco GP victory in 1969.

Lotus 72

This was to serve Team Lotus from 1970 until 1975, winning 20 Grands Prix in the hands of Jochen Rindt, Emerson Fittipaldi and Ronnie Peterson, and the Constructors' Championship in 1970, 1972 and 1973.

It stood out for its overall wedge lines, with a fine nose and hip radiators alongside the rear of the cockpit, there was torsion bar suspension, and

Above: Emerson Fittipaldi in an early Lotus 72, showing its trend-setting wedge lines (and in this case an enormous rear aerofoil). Left: Colin Chapman's team broke new ground with the Lotus 78, using the airflow under the car to vastly improve roadholding. This 78 is being tested at Brands Hatch by Ronnie Peterson.

inboard brakes to keep heat away from soft-compound tyres as well as reduce unsprung weight. Its appearance was to change as new aerodynamic components and engine airboxes were introduced.

Lotus 78 and 79

Once again Chapman looked to originality to restore his Team's fortunes in the late 1970s, and compensate for a power handicap as it was still using DFV engines. The Lotus R&D aero-dynamicists under Peter Wright persevered with ground effects using   der a car to suck it to the track, gaining enormous roadholding and cornering advantages.

This technique was exploited in the 78, which Mario Andretti described as 'painted to the road' and drove to win four GPs. Gunnar Nilsson also won once in a 78, then in 1978 Andretti and Peterson each won a GP in a 78, before the more refined 79 made its debut. Andretti won four GPs in 79s, and took the Drivers' Championship, while Peterson also won in a 79.

Once again the racing world was to follow a Lotus lead, while Team Lotus was to falter. It was to win Grands Prix with turbo cars in the mid-1980s, but too obviously the driving inspiration of Colin Chapman was missing . . .

Above: Mario Andretti and Ronnie Peterson in 1978, both driving Lotus 79 ground effects cars.

Index